SHAMBALA

SHAMBALA

The Constitution of
a Traditional State

by

EDGAR V. WINANS

Foreword by
WALTER GOLDSCHMIDT
Professor of Anthropology and Sociology
University of California

LONDON
ROUTLEDGE & KEGAN PAUL

For Patricia

CONTENTS

Contents

PLATES

N.B. All photographs are by the author.

FOREWORD

WHY and how governments are instituted among men remains one of the most intriguing problems in social philosophy. It has been the subject of enquiry throughout the history of Western civilization. Yet our understanding remains unsatisfactory; our knowledge incomplete.

It is in the modern anthropological tradition to take the empirical view; to look at the actual cases and conditions as demonstrated by the peoples of the world, without any let or hindrance from those cultural predilections and social biases that form part of the anthropologists' own heritage. Thus in the field of political enquiry, as in every other field of human activity from economic life to religious belief, the anthropologists start with the data derived from ethnographic investigation. While the anthropologist cannot observe the actual coming into being of a governmental system, he does have the opportunity to examine the nascent aspects of political activities; he does see institutions of government in something comparable to their primordial condition.

To the anthropological study of political systems, Africa represents a natural laboratory. For among the peoples of sub-Saharan Africa were to be found the widest possible range in the development of the institutions of governance, from the smallest bands of Bushmen and Pygmy to such great political systems as the Baganda, Ashanti, and Dahomey. In the past two decades there have expectably been several works dealing with the institutions of government in native Africa.

The Shambalai are one African political system organized as a state, and Professor Winans here gives us a clear and detailed analysis of the structure and functioning of that system. Thus, the volume adds to our empirical knowledge of primitive political life. But the present study does more than offer us an analysis of a political structure; it gives us insights which can significantly further our understanding of the character of political institutions. It is precisely because *Shambala: The Constitution of a Traditional State* offers as such insights into the origin

xi

and character of state systems that I was most happy to accept Professor Winans' invitation to write this Foreword.

Though anthropology, since its very inception, has concerned itself with the institutions of government among non-literate societies, its contribution to political theory is meager in the extreme. The paucity of theory in the anthropological vein can easily be demonstrated. In 1861, Sir Henry Maine developed the distinction between 'societas' and 'civitas', between the community organized upon a personal, kinship basis and the community organized territorially through institutions of government which maintain order by the administration of laws. Influenced by the then current older evolutionary theory, Maine was primarily concerned with the evolution of the former into the latter.

In 1940, Meyer Fortes and E. E. Evans-Pritchard edited a volume of descriptive summaries of political institutions of eight African peoples. Their introduction to this volume centers on a distinction between two types: 'One group . . . consists of those societies which has centralized authority, administrative machinery, and judicial institutions . . . The other group . . . consists of those societies which lack centralized authority, administrative machinery, and constituted judicial institutions . . .' Later on they say: 'In the societies of Group A, it is the administrative organization, in the societies of Group B, the segmentary lineage system, which regulates political relations between territorial segments.' [1]

Clearly the eighty years that intervened between these two works did not bring about any marked progress in the taxonomy of political institutions. It is fair to say that the difference between these two works lies largely in the idiom in which the categories are expressed, for whereas Maine wrote in terms of origins, development, and evolution, Fortes and Evans-Pritchard wrote in terms of institutions and social relationships.

In the remaining twenty years of the century that has passed since Maine wrote *Ancient Law*, scholars have paid increasing attention to the theory and character of primitive government, especially in Africa. Among the more important descriptive

[1] Meyer Fortes and E. E. Evans-Pritchard, 1940, pp. 5–6.

summaries have been those by Barnes on the Ngoni of Northern Rhodesia and Nyasaland, by Southall on the Alur and Fallers on the Soga (both in Uganda), and by M. G. Smith on the Hausa Chiefdom of Zazzau.[1] Each of these works, though primarily descriptive, has been concerned with the broader theoretical implications that their analyses have for the understanding of political institutions in general. In addition, statements by Brown, Kaberry, and Eisenstadt have endeavored to further understanding of political systems on a comparative basis.[2]

It seems to me that the slow rate of progress in developing an anthropological theory of government has derived from the failure to ask the right questions of the data. The questions that underlie Professor Winans' analysis of Shambala political structure are functional ones: Which functions must a social system have if it is to operate as a unified and coherent whole? Which problems must be resolved for the maintenance of such a unit? To such broad and general questions the anthropologist concerned with Africa must add: Which special problems emerge in a non-literate society from the very absence of writing, and how are these met? Which special problems exist in nascent state systems where the advantages of large-scale cooperation are not visible to the rank and file of the population, and where there is no tradition upon which to base political unity?

In such reformulation of the questions, we have subtly but significantly changed the nature of our enquiry. For our questions are directed to the functional requisites for a system of governance rather than to the structural characteristics of the institutions of government. We are not concerning ourselves primarily with the nature of entities, but rather with the jobs that must be done. Anthropologists have been prone to view political institutions—and indeed, all institutions—in terms of structural units. What we should do instead is to concentrate on the functional element: the things that get done and the things that *must* get done if there is to be a viable state. This point is forcibly made by Gabriel Almond in his introduction to *The Politics of Developing Areas*, when he asks for a comparative

---

[1] Barnes, 1954; Southall, 1956; Fallers, 1956; Smith, 1960.
[2] Brown, 1951; Kaberry, 1957; Eisenstadt, 1959.

'physiology' rather than a comparative 'anatomy' of political structures.[1]

Let us dwell for a moment on the implications of the word 'must' in the preceding paragraph, for in that monosyllable lies a great deal of implicit theory, as I have noted elsewhere.[2] Man is committed to social existence by the nature of his physical needs; but this commitment places each individual in the dilemma of self-interest versus social demand. Society must provide orderly processes for the regular resolution of this inherent conflict, if the society is to continue. The 'must' therefore has no reference to moral requisites, nor to inevitability, but rather to survival. *If* the society is to continue as a society, *then* it must have certain organizational features. The precise nature of these features will vary from one society to another; that is, these functions may be performed by variant structural elements. But the functions must be performed, or the society will cease to exist. This is true for all societies, however primitive or developed; it is also true for societies of a particular character, and the range of organizational choices are therewith narrowed. We shall see that the special demands of statehood make certain organizational features necessary, if the state is to exist as an entity.

We are therefore concerned with the functions which must be performed in a state system, if that system is to resist the sources of disruption both from within and from without. To Western man, who has been habituated for centuries to take political integration for granted, the question may seem academic. Our students of political behavior have concerned themselves largely with the variant modes of organization; their weaknesses and their strength. But the anthropologist, concerned with social systems in the broader context, is faced with the question: Why have political integration at all? Or again, in order to have political integration, what special functions must be performed in a society that lacks writing (and hence documents), centralized economic industries (and thus manifest economic advantages), an effective weapon technology (and thus a serious difficulty in concentrating power), and other such elements that

[1] Gabriel Almond and James S. Coleman, eds., *The Politics of Developing Areas*, 1960, p. 13.
[2] Goldschmidt, 1959, chap. III.

tend to give support to modern unified political systems. It is in terms of such questions and their answers that we can attack the central question of political discourse: What institutional devices appear to be necessary to a nascent state? The analysis in *Shambala: The Constitution of a Traditional State* provides us with the opportunity to see the answers to such questions as they apply to a single political system.

I should now like to discuss the functional requisites of a state system under three major headings: legitimacy, articulation, and self-maintenance; to illustrate these with the Shambala evidence recorded here by Winans; and occasionally to invoke a few well-known examples for comparative purposes.

Legitimacy has two separate but interrelated aspects: it involves the recognition of the rights of the rulers to rule, of the government to operate. It involves also the commitment on part of the population to accept the rulers and their modes of operation. We recall that in the Declaration of Independence its framers were early constrained to express the legitimacy of government, using the Lockean phraseology: 'deriving their just powers from the consent of the governed.' Earlier European states had defined the right to rule as a divine one, though this legitimacy had long been questioned and the rule subordinated in Western Europe.

The legitimacy of Shambala government is established in what must be accepted as a kind of historical myth: the Mbega Myth. This myth not only provides a justification for the distinction between the royal Kilindi clan and the rank and file population, but it also justifies their rule as having been sought out by the people, and provides a blueprint for the very structuring of authority. Its mythic form makes it a twice-told tale, ready on the lips of the learned if not of the ordinary man. To American ears it provides a kind of constitution for the state itself, but it is doubtless more appropriate to call it a charter, as Winans has done, following the British-influenced terminology of Malinowski. In the absence of writing, it is difficult to conceive of a better means of documenting a system of government than through such a tale, bearing as it does the dual sanctions of history (however perverted from actual events it may be) and of religious belief.

Yet we must remember that a myth can be either altered or left aside; it does not in itself provide for that sense of individual commitment on the part of the rank and file which is necessary for the maintenance of large-scale political organizations made up, as Shambalai was, of diverse cultural elements and of a population so numerous that the people could not relate to one another on a personal, face-to-face basis. To this end there evolved among the Shambala a second device, less direct but equally effective and important. This was the initiation ritual. This ritual appears to be an expression of allegiance to the state itself, a personal but public acceptance by the common man of the royal prerogative to rule. What appears to have happened is that the various clans gave up their own initiation rites and adopted those of the Kilindi clan. In so doing, they submitted in fact and in sentiment to the royal clan and gave reality to the charter provided by the Mbega myth. One can hardly escape feeling that originally the prestige of the royal group, as it was spreading its influence and power throughout Shambalai, made its ceremonies desirable to the subordinate groups, and their adoption of the ceremonies became a means of acknowledgement. However the practice emerged, it served as an expression of individual allegiance to the Kilindi rule. Winans found that the Shambala provided us with a kind of test of this, an exception that proves the rule. The fact that the one clan that failed to accept the initiation ceremony managed to retain a much greater independence from Kilindi rule makes this functional role very clear. Specifically, members of this clan who accepted the Kilindi initiation were considered to have expressly shifted their loyalties from the highly independent clan to the Shambala state.

The second functional requisite of a state system is organization, or what I would prefer to call articulation. A state is made up of many entities, and if it is to be a state, these entities must be integrated into some larger units in such a way that there is coordination of action. Furthermore, this articulation must be consistent and sufficiently evident that its operations are visible to the community as a whole.

In the Western tradition, we are prone to view this articulation process as inevitably being understood through spatial

entities—wards, parishes, counties, districts, and the like. Such
a system has its natural advantages, particularly among a
people tied closely to the land. It is also found among primitive
peoples. But it is by no means the only way in which the diverse
and dispersed population of a political entity may be joined
together. The Shambalai articulated their state in a different
way; they chose the idiom of kinship to establish the order of
segments to one another in a hierarchy ascending through three
levels to the paramount chief. People were grouped in terms
of kin units rather than geographic ones. The justification for
this system lies, of course, in the Mbega myth itself. But the
important point is that kinship has been used as the means for
providing bureaucratic structures through which unity of action
(and hence the state itself) is maintained. Certainly the Shambala are not unique in this. Ashanti is the classic example of
the use of this principle; and it is in fact a frequent element
in the structuring of African states.

The essential elements in the structuring of social action in
Shambalai are the following: (1) a separation of the ruling clan
from the commoner population, (2) the hierarchy of officialdom
built on a genealogical blueprint involving three separate
organizational levels, (3) the treatment of commoner lineages
as unitary legal entities, and (4) the special relationship between
the commoner lineage unit and the hierarchy of royal chiefs.
The system worked in such a way that the structuring of
authority was clear; it articulated every individual to the whole
and made for a direct and explicit chain of command.

We have already noted the superstructure of political
organization established through the recognition of the royal
clan and its internal hierarchy. The problem of articulation to
the rank and file is a delicate one, but it too is clearly delineated.
The common man is attached to the system through his lineage,
for it appears that in the legal fiction of the Shambala state,
only the lineage exists as a jural entity. Lineage heads control
the internal affairs of their units, and they relate to the royal
chiefs in that they (*a*) take a positive role in the selection of the
chief among those eligible to rule and (*b*) serve as council to the
chiefs. Thus each person relates to the whole through his lineage spokesman. It is worth noting that whether or not the
assertion in the Mbega myth, that the local people sought their

Kilindi rulers, is true, the myth does reflect the sociology of the present day situation, in that the lineages choose and guide their royal chiefs.

This system is reinforced by ritual. For the pattern of ancestor worship requires the ritual subordination of individuals to superiors of their group in such a way as to re-enact their secular subordination, thereby giving religious reaffirmation to the authority of the lineage head.

Institutions of self-maintenance are required in every society, but they are particularly important in state systems, where the diversity of cultural backgrounds and the differences in social rewards are apt to disrupt social unity. Of the many facets of self-maintenance, we will discuss the following: the need for protection from outsiders, the provision of machinery for maintaining and restoring order within the system, the orderly transfer of powers, and the support of public institutions and public works.

The existence of military institutions provides the means of protection against outsiders. The Shambala state had no standing army, but it did have a call upon the citizenry. Apparently, it was also possible for individuals to establish military units in order to subordinate neighboring peoples, but it is not clear what controls the paramount chief exerted over such activities. It does appear, however, that Shambala military prowess was under the control of the central government.

Threats from the outside were a lesser problem in the maintenance of Shambala social order than internal political disruption. Any social system must provide for the restitution of order when the conduct of its constituent members endangers its continued unity by denial of established moral order or by disputation, by quarrels, or by infringements upon the recognized rights of fellow citizens. In a society organized as a state, the essential machinery must be provided by the government and must be under its control. For the state cannot tolerate that individuals or groups in the society regularly undertake on their own the use of force to protect their own rights against others in the system. Indeed, this follows from the basic definition of a state; namely, that the government holds a monopoly on the legitimate use of force.

Foreword

The genealogically-based Shambala bureaucracy served as court. This court system did not recognize the individual; it tried matters between lineages. The internal structure of the lineage was familistic; its head had the power of adjudication and punishment within the family unit. However, an act of any lineage member which allegedly brought harm to a person from another lineage was a matter for the court system, and the lineage as a whole, represented by its head, was under trial. The council of lineage heads, together with the chief of jurisdiction from the royal clan, determined fault and assessed penalty. Presumably the several levels in the chiefly hierarchy provided an appeal system (this matter is not entirely clear) so that ultimate decision rested upon the head of the state. From this it is seen that the political structure as such held the ultimate power over all disputes taking place within its jurisdiction, except those internal to the localized lineage.

Any social system involving a series of offices must face the problem of succession. The orderly transfer of office from an incumbent to his successor forms a natural point of weakness in any political organization. Leaving aside the problems inherent in modern democratic selection and focusing upon monarchical government, there is a built-in dilemma in the processes of succession to kingship and other high office. A system like the British monarchy, which provides an absolute line of succession, has no technique for eliminating the relatively weak and unfit (though where the monarch is but a symbol, this is not a serious defect). A system that leaves succession open to choice provides a basis for sharp internecine conflict whenever transfer of power becomes necessary. Either course leaves the society vulnerable; there is no true solution to this dilemma, but only compromise.

An examination of the Baganda pattern is enough to convince one of the difficulties that can ensue when a society fails to develop an adequate solution to this problem. The Baganda had one of the most closely-knit and highly-organized state systems known to ethnology, and yet it seems never to have achieved a stable means of succession to the Kabakaship, so that whenever a Kabaka died there was a marked disruption in the orderly process of public life.[1]

[1] Roscoe, 1911.

The Shambala found a more satisfactory compromise of this inherent dilemma. Chiefly office was restricted to the royal lineage, and this privilege was supported by what Winans calls 'a belief in the inborn fitness of the ruling class to rule'. Flexibility was maintained by a rather wide choice from among the eligible class. Yet disruption was prevented by the importance of the role in the selection played by the council of commoners, which represented the constituency of the office to be filled. The council had the legal right to nominate candidates; the royal clan to accept or veto such nomination. In a very real sense, the Shambala structure provided for democratic selection, despite its elitist bias; and this popular voice must have played an important role in maintaining the integrity of the state and the loyalty of its rank and file.

A closely related potential source of disruption in any political system lies in the accumulation of a disaffected cadet sector, whose political ambitions are frustrated by the differential between the birth rate and the incidence of opportunity. The Shambala were to no little extent protected against this threat by their own expansionist tendencies, which gave opportunity to the ambitious members of the royal clan to establish power over peripheral areas. This expansionism not only prevented disruption, but also increased the scope of the state itself. Court intrigue and questions of succession appear to have remained minimal, a state of affairs that must be credited in part to the opportunity for expansion. It is a solution not unknown to Western society.

Finally, self-maintenance requires the economic support of the authority system. Shambalai was not marked by public works. Aside from a system of roads and trails, and the moderately elaborate courts of the officialdom, there were no major expenditures of time and resources. But despite the modest scale of the court system, there nevertheless had to be some means of taxation and corvée if these minimal amenities were to be preserved. The assertion that taxes are as certain as death may not be true; nonetheless they are an essential ingredient in a state system of society. Perhaps some anthropologists would evoke the League of the Iroquois, but an examination of the League convinces one that not only did it fail to provide public works, but it did not control an army and did not develop a judicial system. In short, it was not a true state; it was merely a confederation—an institutionalized truce—serving the common interests of the several truly sovereign tribes.

We have pointed up some of the requisite elements of a state: the need for a charter to provide legitimacy to the personnel and procedures of rulership, and the counterpart of this, an expression of commitment—of citizenship—by the rank and file; the provision of a systematic organization, clear and visible to everyone and elaborated enough to provide an articulation of all parts to the whole; and institutional features for self maintenance, including the provision of an army as protection against the outside, of a judicial system as protection against internal dissent, of orderly succession to office, and of the flow of goods and services requisite to the physical needs of the state itself.

We may now return to the distinction between state and non-state organized societies, which was first formulated by Sir Henry Maine, and which remains current in the literature of anthropology today—though it is not without its critics. Is this distinction, then, a valid one? I think it is, but I do not think it has been adequately comprehended. States are forms of social systems which meet special circumstances and which have special requirements—and, it should be said, special potentialities. They are characterized by institutional devices, such as those which have been described by Winans for the Shambala, and which we have summarized above.

Those who take the opposite viewpoint see in the organization of government the expansion outward of the controls inherent in all social systems. They see, as did MacIver and Lowie,[1] the origin of political institutions in family law, which has extended to the whole of society. There is a certain validity in this viewpoint, though perhaps not quite in the way these authors intend. The controls of political systems are often, if not always, a psychologic extrapolation from the intimate experiences of domestic life. And it may also be correct that political institutions have been an evolutionary development out of earlier familistic types of social control. But neither psychological nor evolutionary continuity is really in point. The

[1] MacIver, 1947; Lowie, 1927.

essence of all evolutionary development is that, however gradual may be the process of change, ultimately a truly new form emerges, with distinctive elements; and that this new form creates new potentialities for social life. It is such with the distinction between tribe and state. This distinction is of such fundamental importance to the understanding of social systems that we must explore it in some detail.

First, we must distinguish two words that have already been used: government and governance. By the latter I mean the regularized procedures and practices for maintaining an orderly way of life among a population; by the former I mean the specific organization of offices, of powers, of social roles, and the like which exist for the purpose of maintaining order and compliance among a people. Governance is the function of maintaining harmony; government the structure by which that function may be performed. Governance is universal among men; governments are found only among some peoples. To appreciate this distinction, we must make certain others.

The first of these distinctions is between internal and external order. By internal order, I mean the order that prevails within a group; the rules by which its members abide because of their commitment to the group and their recognition of the authority of the existing powers within it. The group may be a family, a band, a tribe, or a nation. It has an internal structure, and within it there is order and authority—a decision-making power. By external order I mean the order that prevails between two or more such groups because of their adherence to common rules and common procedures, but where there is no recognized authority or force to which these groups submit. There is order because they adhere to common values and principles, because they obey common laws, and because, when disputes arise, they recognize common procedures for the adjudication of conflict. But they do not recognize that any person or group has the power to determine the fault and assess the penalty. There is no hierarchy of powers, but each unit is potentially a free agency. (There is, of course, a third level, where no common values, principles, rules, or procedures exist. Under such circumstances, there is no order at all.)

It will readily be seen that this distinction is based upon another, extremely important one; namely, the agency by which disputes are settled. Essentially there are two: (1) the parties to the dispute themselves, or (2) a third party. Within an internally-ordered group there will be a third party decision; where there is only external order, the punishment of the infraction is the responsibility of the injured party—though if there is to be order, it must operate within the framework of established procedures.

Finally, we must distinguish between law and government. We are so used to thinking of law as the product of government that we often doubt that the former can exist without the latter —forgetting that our own law derives ultimately from ancient tribal customs. Yet laws exist among primitive peoples without governments. Indeed, there are tribes, such as the Yurok of California and the Ifugao of the Philippine Islands,[1] in which the laws are so explicit that they are all but codified, though there is no law enforcement agency whatsoever. Not all primitive law is as explicit as this; nevertheless, a body of basic doctrine and of legal procedure is regularly found.

Now on the basis of these distinctions, it is possible to formulate the difference between tribal and state social systems. A tribal society is one in which internal order prevails only on a familistic or other limited basis, but where such units are brought together (and share a common territory) under a system of external order, so that legal procedures are based upon the direct actions of the principals to a dispute, and are not adjudicated by a third party that is given the power of determining guilt and assessing indemnity.

Let us see how this works. In a clan-organized society such as the Tlingit Indians of Southeastern Alaska, there is no governmental organization whatsoever.[2] The whole Tlingit are divided into a series of tribes or territories, but these smaller units also have no political institutions. The order is maintained through kinship unities, which are not bounded by space and not independent of one another. The Tlingit people are divided into two intermarrying, exogamous moieties. Each person is a member of that of his mother. They are further divided into matrilineal clans. These groupings extend throughout the tribe. The clans in turn fall into housegroups, large extended matrilineal subdivisions of the clan, made up of several nuclear

---

[1] Kroeber, 1925, 1926; Barton, 1915.   [2] Oberg, 1934, 1937.

families. Each person is therefore a member of a nuclear family, a house-group, a clan, and a moiety. There is a kind of informal hierarchy, with house-group chiefs, clan heads, and perhaps (it is not entirely clear) moiety leaders. Now housegroup and clan have internal order (perhaps to a limited extent the moiety also), but the tribe has none. If a dispute arises between persons of two separate clans, there is only one way to adjudicate matters—through negotiation between the clan leaders. These may endeavor to find a solution along established procedural lines and agree on a settlement. But behind such disputes—the sanction for law, if you wish—lies recourse to arms. As the Ifugao put it in their even less organized but comparable system, behind every dispute stands the lance. Though it might be appropriate to think of the clans as having a government, the tribe does not; and it is important to appreciate the fact that the clan is not an independent, self-standing entity. For the clan is a family; its members are, by the rule of exogamy, married to other clans, and these clans are also interdependent in economic, social, and ritual functions. It is fair to say that each clan is a sovereign entity in regular intercourse and in close interrelations with other similar sovereign clans; that in the ordinary course of events these work and play together, but that their unity is by mutual consent and not through the recognition of a common overriding power.

The contrast with the Shambala—and hence between tribe and state—should be clear. Though the Shambala have both lineages and clans, and though the former have an internal authority within which government does not intervene, these units are clearly subordinated to a dominant structure in all matters arising between separate such units. There is a larger internal order, with third-party legal decisions recognized and submitted to; there is government.

What emerges from this discussion is that governmental structures in state systems have a monopoly on the legitimate use of force, and that it is precisely in the absence of such powers that the tribal societies are distinct from states. This, it should be noted, is the definition of a state expressed by Max Weber and subsequently used by most writers on political institutions. And, we should further note, to have a monopoly on the use of force requires institutions of adjudication, for in their absence, force must be used directly by the rank and file. If courts are to function under the stress of disputes, then they must be recognized as legitimate, they must be articulated into a whole, and there must be a hierarchy of personnel to administer to them. The verbal identity in English (and other European languages) between court as the seat of government and court as the adjudicative mechanism is no accident. They are, in fact and in essence, one and the same thing.

Another point of importance emerges from this redefinition of the distinction between tribal and state societies. Older writers have asserted that the two were distinct, in that tribal societies were based upon kinship roles, whereas states were based upon official roles; that one was mechanical, the other organic (to use Durkheim's phrasing). This is essentially the basis of the dichotomy both of Maine and of Evans-Pritchard and Fortes. But clearly the Shambala have a state, yet it is articulated almost wholly on a kinship principle. This is true of other primitive states, and therefore they cannot be distinguished on the basis of this structural feature. It is true that state organized social systems do not usually place as much emphasis upon kinship as do most tribally organized societies, but this is in reality a secondary consequence. Organizing society on the basis of kinship—even articulated through clans—tends to make matters personal and individual. It is a system that works satisfactorily only with rather small numbers. But governmental structures exist precisely because they coordinate large bodies of people into a single system—too large a number to operate on so personal and individual a basis. For this reason there is a strain to substitute specific roles (offices) for kin relationships through which to organize action. Yet Shambalai indicates that this is not necessary for a small state, and some primitive societies establish a kind of fictive kin in the hierarchy of offices. It is fair to say, however, that there are limits beyond which the operations of the kinship principle cannot go, that no modern state is so organized, and that this has been true in the West since antiquity.

While the distinction between tribal and state societies is real and important, we must recognize also that it is not pure. Certainly there are anticipations of statehood among tribal peoples, there are borderline cases, and there are states that are not fully realized. From an evolutionary point of view, such circumstances are to be expected.

Among tribal societies we find institutions of governance which allow for a degree of control by some person or sector over a broad population. The Plains Indians policing societies were precisely such. During the buffalo hunt, these societies had control over the whole camp and could enforce their rules. Among the Zuñi and other Pueblos, the priesthood appears to have exerted a rather close secular control. Among the Masai of East Africa and neighboring Nandi-speaking peoples, a 'rain-maker' or religious leader appears also to have had much secular influence. But his jurisdiction was uncertain, his authority limited, and his power dependent upon his psychological and mystic appeals. Such systems cannot be called states (though they provide for a measure of control and regularity) because there is no true monopoly on the legitimate use of force.

Elsewhere we have political institutions in the form of a chief who acts as judge over a recognized jurisdiction. The Ba-Ila chief, for example, adjudicated disputes, but only within the limits of his own small community.[1] Furthermore, disputants apparently could operate through clans and take recourse in arms, and so by-pass the chief. The small principalities of the Soga also seem very limited in scope, though Fallers sees them as small states, since there existed a royal class articulated to commoner lineage through a pattern of clientship, and this royalty held power over the peasants through a legitimate structure of authority.[2] Compared to their massive and better-articulated neighbors, the Nyoro and the Baganda, the Soga states are very small and weak. The Soga certainly did not derive the full potentialities of political organization.

Many African states operate on a fundamentally feudal pattern. That is, the ruling class articulates through clients who are, in turn, overlords of a district or area. Between king and client there is a mutual relationship; between client and peasants a master-serf relationship. Such is the pattern among the Ankole of Uganda and other Interlacustrine Bantu.[3] The overlords are militaristic cattle-owners and the serfs are farmers. Such feudal relationships—operating more with respect to

[1] Smith and Dale, 1920.   [2] Fallers, 1956.   [3] Oberg, 1940.

cattle than to territory—offer a mode of articulation different from the kinship pattern of the Shambalai or the territorial structure that characterizes Western political organization. Many writers have seen in feudalism a form of primitive political development, an inadequately realized state. Certainly the feudal structure does not make for the degree of stability and unity that we take to be essential for nationhood today.

The Ba-Ila, the Soga and the Ankole, it seems to me, represent unfulfilled political forms; they lack the stability and the power of true states. This is not true of all African states. Perhaps the most fully realized political system in the eastern portion of Africa was that of Buganda, the kingdom on the north shores of Lake Victoria.[1] Buganda held together a wide territory and a large population by means of a strong ruler and an elaborate and closely-knit bureaucracy. One of its most unusual features was the degree to which the ranks of officialdom, extending down to the village level, were controlled from above. The system articulated entirely through spatial entities —counties, sub-counties, villages—over which appointed officials held wide administrative and adjudicative power. Administrative loyalty was to the Kabaka, not to the constituency, for appointments came from the central organization. Except, perhaps, for the lack of clear rules of succession (which has already been alluded to) it was probably the most highly centralized and completely realized political system found among an unlettered people.

One cannot read the literature of Baganda political structure without being struck by one point which, I believe, has pertinence to the development of political institutions. The whole institutional system of government under the royal leadership of the Kabaka, with its bureaucratic hierarchy of dependent offices, appears to have been in strong and successful competition with the clans for establishing power. The Kabaka was insistent that both land ownership and adjudicative processes were in his hands, and the data suggest that both were once in the hands of the clan leaders. Though clans had been co-opted into government by giving their leaders special prerogatives, there appears to have been much tension between the two orders of leadership. It is difficult not to think of the state system

[1] Roscoe, 1911.

as having superseded an older tribal type of organization in Buganda.

In Ashanti, the political unity is built on the older lineage and clan system.[1] That is, the superstructure continues the principle of lineage loyalty into ever higher units until it attains the level of the Ashanti kingdom as a whole and reaches the person of the Asantahene. It is a federation, and Ashanti traditions support the assumption that it has been built on an older tribal system. Again, during the 19th century the Ngoni built a kind of roving kingdom, with political controls by a central authority. Here a governmental structure came into being and had a short eventful life, exploiting a wide area of Southern Africa and its inhabitants.

We have stopped to discuss these variant political forms for several reasons. First, they show us that there are diverse ways in which primitive states may structure their authority. They may use spatial, feudal patronship, or kinship principles of structure, or some combination of these. Second, they indicate that power varies both in its geographical range and in the range of actions covered. Finally, we gain some insight from these examples into the nature of that twilight zone between tribal societies and fully functioning state organizations. Governmental organization is an institutional means of increasing the power of a society, but it contains its own sources of internal disruption. Under primitive conditions people seem to cross the line between tribal and state organization frequently, but they are not always able to sustain the latter. Some peoples, like the Ba-Ila, seem to have lost their more developed political institutions, while others, like the Shambala, retain much of the older tribal institutional structure in their state system. This is not so much shown by their use of the kinship idiom for structuring the political hierarchy as it is by the continued legal and social importance of the lineage and the powers of the lineage in political life. Though states have long existed in the Shambala area, the Shambala themselves consider their political unity to be new; and the character of Shambala political institutions indicates that, though certainly Shambalai is a state and not a tribal society, it may well be called nascent.

---

[1] Rattray, 1929; Busia, 1951.

It is proper to ask: Why have a state system, rather than a tribal one? The evolutionary point of view suggests that it is better—not better in any moral sense, nor even explicitly from the increased satisfactions of its people, but only in the sense of being better fitted for continued existence in the world under the circumstances in which it appeared. What, we may ask, does the Shambala citizen gain by recognition of an elite and the acceptance of its right to rule; what does he get in return for his taxes and his labor, his tribute and his deference? Does he accept the Mbega myth because he is gullible and the initiation because he wishes to identify psychologically with the heroes of this tale? Is the system accepted, in other words, because it is there? Though the Shambala cannot answer these questions for us, I think they deserve our consideration.

What are the possible motivations and forces that make for the acceptance of an orderly political system despite its costs and its disadvantages? First, a people may accept the political super-structure because it is forced to, as in a conquest state. This does not appear to have been the case in Shambalai; the Mbega myth asserts the opposite, and the events seem to me to be too recent to allow a conquest history to have been so thoroughly obscured. A second force lies in the potentiality of large-scale public works. Modern states are requisite, for our technology (which, to be sure, could only develop under the aegis of large-scale political institutions) requires the peaceable collaboration of large bodies of people. If our political unity were to fail, our whole way of life would be disrupted. This factor has increasingly been of importance to the Western World, and it provides a rationale for state systems where irrigation is important.[1] But neither advanced technology nor irrigation were found in Shambalai; it is doubtful whether the economic pattern and productivity was in any important respect different than it would have been if the Shambala had lived in a tribal system.

A state may be a profitable venture if it is itself a conquest organization. Baganda life was considerably enriched by a flow of goods and services from neighbors into its kingdom—though we may question how widely the profits from such ventures was shared. The Aztecs, we will recall, considered themselves idle when not at war, and this for the good economic reason that

[1] Wittfogel, 1957.

war was a more profitable business for the citizen of Tenoch-
titlan than was farming. The Aztec citizens had good reasons
to support their state organization. Among the Shambala,
though there was some conquest and tribute, it was not at such
a level as to afford much aid and comfort to the citizenry, but
only to the royal clan.

There remains, however, the obverse of this coin: mutual
protection. Two interrelated elements in East Africa made
unified action advantageous to the population as a whole.
Shambalai lies close to the Arab dominated coast, and there is
little doubt that the Shambala were prey to the unified forces
of coastal peoples with their superior technology and greater
resources. Furthermore, it lay in the area of heavy slave trading;
the unity of Shambala was a positive protection against the real
and potential depredations of slave traders. Herein lay, it seems
to me, the only true advantage of political unity to the ordinary
citizen. It is an advantage that the villager shared with his
superiors.

In all this it must be recognized that statehood and the
political hierarchy fell lightly on the shoulders of the Shambalai
citizen; or so I read the data. There was no harsh and autocratic
rule; there were no heavy taxes nor heavy and onerous public
duties of a kind that have made a political superstructure a
burden to the citizen in other places. If the state provided little
but protection from outside forces, it demanded little in return
in the ordinary course of events—though, apparently, the
ruling group did from time to time enforce sudden and un-
expected demands on the wealthy commoners.

There is one further point here. As we have noted, the genius
of Shambalai, despite its elitist tradition, despite its incipient
caste system, was highly democratic. At every crucial juncture,
the citizens (through their lineage heads) had an important say
in matters of government. If only members of the elite class
could aspire to important office, the commoner groups nevertheless had a determining influence upon just who might hold
the office, and in this they were in large measure insured against
malfeasance and oppression. In court decisions, it was their
voice that set the tone of the decisions rendered, even though
such decisions were ultimately enunciated by the royalty as a
royal prerogative. And in domestic affairs, in matters internal

to a lineage, the ordinary citizen was supreme; the officials provided by the state held no powers over the ordinary man in his domestic life.

All this is no accident. The Mbega myth is specific on this point; the power of the leaders was not imposed. It was given by the citizenry who wanted the leadership that Mbega and his relatives could provide. Examine the ritual of coronation for the British ruling monarch, and you will find the same thing symbolized—the subordination of his Royal Majesty to the will of the people. Examine the constitution of the United States, and you will find that the concentration of power—the military —is directly under the President, who is responsible to the people. The charters for these societies provide for the subordination of leadership to the popular will.

It is of particular interest to find such a democratic charter and such democratic institutions in a primitive state. Shambalai was in a very real sense a democratic state. This is not true of all primitive political states, though this is not to say that Shambalai was unique. Why Shambalai should have been democratic is not entirely clear. Perhaps it is because it was not originally a conquest state; perhaps because the advantages to the rank and file of state organization were not very great and they would therefore not submit to such dominance; and perhaps it stems from some deep cultural source in the attitudes and sentiments of the people themselves.

The evolution of social organization must be seen as a gradual development, with many variant solutions to the problem of maintaining order. Yet, as in all evolutionary matters, there comes the point of break-through—the emergence of a means by which new levels of accomplishment may be attained. The emergence of statehood was one such development. It must have occurred many times among many peoples, and in its early stages need not have been of very great advantage. The study of African political systems shows us something of the character that statecraft must have had under these early circumstances, though they themselves do not go back to that early beginning. They show us also the essential elements of statehood and the institutional problems that political systems must face if they are to be retained. And while Shambalai cannot be regarded as a well-developed political system, while it does not appear to have had great strength and power, yet it does have a certain quality of equity and good will; it does have a nice balance between unity and freedom, between authority and democracy, between practicality and sentiment.

Shambala: The Constitution of a Traditional State affords us insight into the character of primitive political organizations. It is through the description and analysis of such systems that we can comprehend the meaning of statehood and the problems of primitive statecraft. And by a better understanding of the functional aspects of political systems, we can gain insight into the evolution of political development.

This evolutionary development is not done. The Shambala are now caught in larger social unities, as befits the economic potentials and social requirements of an industrial order. This is an inevitable development, though it need not inevitably have taken the form it did. One can hope that the leadership that emerges in Tanganyika in the years to come will build their institutions in the context of local heritage. They will do well to look for inspiration to the political order of one society within their territory in the formulation of those institutions necessary for what lies before them.

WALTER GOLDSCHMIDT

February, 1961

BIBLIOGRAPHY

ALMOND, GABRIEL A., and COLEMAN, JAMES S., *The Politics of the Developing Areas*. Princeton: Princeton University Press (1960).

BARNES, J. A., *Politics in a Changing Society: A Political History of the Fort Jameson Ngoni*. London: Oxford University Press (1954).

BARTON, R. F., *Ifugao Law*. Berkeley, University of California Publications in American Archeology and Ethnology, Vol. 15, No. 1 (1919).

BROWN, PAULA, 'Patterns of Authority in West Africa', *Africa*, Vol. 21, 261–78 (1951).

BUSIA, K. A., *The Position of the Chief in the Modern Political System of the Ashanti*. London: Oxford University Press (1951).

EISENSTADT, S. N., 'Primitive Political Systems: A Preliminary Comparative Analysis', *American Anthropologist*, Vol. 61, 2:200–20 (1951).

FALLERS, LLOYD A., *Bantu Bureaucracy, A Study of Integration and Conflict in the Political Institutions of an East African People*. Cambridge: Heffer and Sons (1956).

Bibliography

FORTES, M., 'The Structure of Unilinear Descent Groups', *American Anthropologist*, Vol. 55, No. 1 (1953).

FORTES, M. and EVANS-PRITCHARD, E. E. *African Political Systems*. London: Oxford University Press (1940).

GOLDSCHMIDT, WALTER, *Man's Way, A Preface to the Understanding of Human Society*. New York, Holt-Dryden. *Understanding Human Society*. London, Routledge & Kegan Paul (1960).

KABERRY, PHYLLIS, 'Primitive States'. *The British Journal of Sociology*, Vol. VIII, 3:224–34 (1957).

KROEBER, A. L., *Handbook of the Indians of California*. Bul. 78, Bureau of American Ethnology (1925).

— Law of the Yurok Indians. *Atti del XXII Congreso Internazionale degli Americanisti*, Vol. II (1926).

LOWIE, ROBERT H., *The Origin of the State*. New York: Harcourt Brace & Co. (1927).

MACIVER, ROBERT M., *The Web of Government*. New York, The Macmillan Co. (1947).

MAINE, SIR HENRY, *Primitive Law*. London and New York (various dates).

OBERG, K., 'Crime and Punishment in Tlingit Society', *American Anthropologist*, Vol. 36, No. 2 (1934).

— *The Social Economy of the Tlingit Indians*. Ph.D. Dissertation, University of Chicago (1937).

— 'The Kingdom of Ankole in Uganda, in *African Political Systems* (M. Fortes and E. E. Evans-Pritchard, eds.). London: Oxford University Press (1940).

RATTRAY, R. S., *Ashanti Law and Constitution*. London: Oxford University Press (1929).

ROSCOE, J., *The Baganda*. London: Macmillan and Co. (1911).

SMITH, E. W. and DALE, A. M., *The Ila-Speaking Peoples of Northern Rhodesia*. London: Macmillan and Co. (1920).

SMITH, M. G., *Government in Zazzau, 1800–1950*. London: Oxford University Press (1960).

SOUTHALL, A. W., *Alur Society, A Study in Processes and Types of Domination*. Cambridge: W. Heffer and Sons (1956).

WITTFOGEL, KARL, *Oriental Despotism, A Comparative Study of Total Power*. New Haven: Yale University Press (1957).

PREFACE

THE field work upon which this study is based was carried out by my wife and myself between August, 1956, and August, 1957. Aside from an absence of three weeks while my wife gave birth to a daughter, we spent the whole of this period in the Usambara Mountains. The bulk of my research was conducted from two bases. The first seven months of the study were mainly spent in the northern sector of the mountains where I concentrated my attention on the Mlalo basin which is an area remote from modern communications and extremely densely populated. Approximately the last four months of the study were spent in the south in the vicinity of Vuga, the traditional capital of the Shambala state.

Relatively soon after my arrival in the Usambara Mountains I was fortunate enough to make the acquaintance of Mr. Sozi Kimella Daffa, a young man who became my patient teacher of Swahili, my interpreter of Shambala, clerk, collector of texts, and collaborator in nearly all phases of field work. With Sozi's aid the work was carried out in a combination of English and Swahili and texts were collected in Shambala to be translated in the evenings. I did not find that one year was sufficient time for me to become fluent in Shambala and I take full responsibility for shortcomings and errors which may exist in my understanding of Shambala culture because of my missing of idioms and metaphors which are not readily translatable and which may only be caught after long and deep experience in a language.

The traditional techniques of the anthropologist comprised the primary means of collecting the data of this study. These include open-ended and directed interviews with individuals, observation of social interaction which was usually followed immediately by interviews with participants, the collection of genealogical materials, short biographies of selected informants, the use of detailed questionnaires intended to elicit specific information from certain categories of individuals, the collection of village census materials and the study of government records and published materials. The basis of my approach was to gather information in such a way as to make it possible to identify informants with increasing precision such that their 'representativeness' of some category of Shambala would be known to me. The data derived from intensive work with this carefully selected range of informants could then be checked by questionnaires or directed interviews with other informants, for it was out of the question to use mass survey techniques in a largely pre-literate population.

A study of this kind which focuses upon the indigenous political organization of a group which has been in acculturative contact with European administrations for over seventy years involves certain difficulties of which the reader will quickly become aware through the rapid shifting of tense in the analysis. It has been necessary to talk almost simultaneously about things as they were in the last century and things as they are today in order to present a picture of a system which is in a process of continuous adaptation. The result is a construct, an abstraction from an on-going organization which shows the mark of both German and British philosophies of rule, the heavy impact of western technology, and yet the dominating outlines of its earlier, pre-european form. It is my hope that I have understood the interplay of these several cultures and different time levels sufficiently well to sort them out effectively.

This study depends to a great extent upon the instruction and stimulation I have received from my teachers and colleagues in the Universities where I have studied and worked. At the University of California at Los Angeles I was introduced to anthropology by Professors Ralph Beals, Walter Goldschmidt, William Lessa, Joseph Birdsell, and the late George Brainerd who gave me subtle and crucial guidance in my first fieldwork in Mexico. Of these men, I am especially indebted to my teacher, critic, confessor, and stern taskmaster, Professor Walter Goldschmidt who first directed my interests towards social anthropology and who guided me in the production of an earlier version of this study as my doctoral dissertation. At the University of Washington I gained much valuable assistance and insight from the critical comments and discussion of Professors Fred O. Gearing, Martin Orans, and Simon Ottenberg and from Dr. Phoebe Ottenberg.

Preface

In East Africa, my investigations were greatly facilitated by the staff of the East African Institute of Social Research and in particular by the then Director, Dr. Lloyd A. Fallers, and by the Institute's excellent secretaries Miss Beryl Berrange and Miss Grace Hunter. Dr. Philip Gulliver, then Senior Government Sociologist, was of great help to me in Tanganyika and I owe him and his wife, Pamela, more than I can say for their hospitality and advice. The Tanganyika Government extended me every cooperation and support and the District Commissioner, Lushoto, Mr. Ian Glennie; the District Officers, Mr. John Cook and Mr. Paul Fabian; and Mr. Clive Green, an agriculture officer with a considerable interest in linguistics all accorded me hospitality and invaluable help in the field.

The members of the Usambara Lutheran Mission staff, particularly Pastor and Mrs. Heinrich Waltenberg and Mr. and Mrs. Gerald Goldeen, were extremely hospitable to my wife and myself. They very generously allowed us to use an unoccupied house and in many ways made us welcome, both in Mlalo and Vuga.

I find it difficult to express adequately the extent to which this study depends upon the aid of my wife Patricia. Her help in the collection and analysis of data is attested to in every page of this work.

An anthropologist owes his greatest debt to the people with whom he works. Whatever I am able to say depends upon the good will and friendship of the many Shambala who answered my questions and allowed me to participate in their lives. For this privilege, I thank them. In particular my most profound thanks go to Sultan Kimweri Mputa Magogo, Q.M., Simbamwene of Usambara, Hassani Kiniashi, Zumbe Mkuu of Mlalo, and my good friend Hamisi Kujighana.

Finally, the research embodied in this work was made possible under fellowships granted by the Ford Foundation and the Social Science Research Council and I wish to express my gratitude for their support. The conclusions and opinions expressed are, of course, my own and not necessarily those of the foundations.

Chapter I

INTRODUCTION

T H I S study will concentrate upon the structure of Shambalai, a pre-literate African state. An outstanding attribute of this state is a clear separation of an elite from the rank and file. This elite which forms a royal clan possesses a virtual monopoly of important administrative positions within the state. It also possesses a tradition, and perhaps a reality, of separate origin and history. The maintenance of political authority involves the popular acceptance of the power of the elite and the provision of the elite with a charter, a structure of command, a public image, and sanctions for the maintenance of power.

I am here concerned to show that the kinship system offers a charter for the authority of the royal lineage and also provides the lines of authority and the channels of communication within the Shambala state. This kinship structure and the moral right of the royal lineage to maintain power are expressed in a basic myth of the origin of the state which provides a charter— a sort of constitution—that legitimizes the present structure.

An elaborate ritual acts to reinforce and further to structure the system. The public worship of royal ancestors not only requires submission to existing authority, but also gives public expression to the ongoing structure of authority. In addition to this ancestor worship in which both royal clansmen and commoners participate, there is an initiation ritual which involves a kind of expression of loyalty to the state.

The myth of origin, the royal genealogies, and the ritual of ancestor worship and initiation all focus attention upon the special nature of the elite. Through these its separateness is maintained.

Acceptance of the hegemony of this royal clan binds together a heterogeneous people who are themselves organized in localized patrilineages and who retain traditions of their separate origins. Their acceptance of the royal clan is based on an explicit tradition of the charismatic qualities of the founder of the state and of the inheritance of this charisma by the agnatic descendants of this founder.[1]

The system thus established is stable in the sense that the political institutions are constant. However, the maintenance of these institutions depended importantly upon the existence of a constantly expanding frontier before European contact. The frontier served to relieve certain potential conflicts within the system, particularly by providing opportunity to those individuals within the royal clan who did not stand directly in the line to inherit established chiefships.

The political authority exercised by the royal strata deals with lineages as entities. There is relatively little penetration of royal power into the internal affairs of a commoner lineage. Authority within the lineage operates upon familistic and seniority principles. It is the relations between lineages that are mediated by the chief. The relations of the individual may be viewed in two ways: from the outside, as by a member of another lineage, the individual is seen as a representative of some corporate group; from the inside, he is an individual related in a certain way to each member of the group and thus possessing clear rights and obligations of a detailed nature known intimately to all. These two alternate views may be analytically separated, but they merge to a certain degree in practice since lineages are connected by ties of marriage. Thus even the chief stands in the important relations of sister's son or mother's brother to many commoners. This produces a ramifying network of ties other than rulership between the two strata of Shambala society.

The Leadership Hierarchy

Not only does the power of chiefship treat of commoner lineages as corporate groups, but the relation among chiefs is one of royal lineage to royal lineage. The chieftaincies form a three-step hierarchy of paramount, great, and lesser chiefs which is based upon the process of segmentation in a deep lineage system. The articulation of royal lineages is genealogical, based ultimately

[1] Max Weber, *The Theory of Social and Economic Organization*, translated by A. M. Henderson and Talcott Parsons (Glencoe: The Free Press and the Falcon's Wing Press, 1947), pp. 358–73.

2

upon the legendary account of the founding of the royal clan. The development of the state is seen by the Shambala as a process of splitting off of sons or brothers of a chief, who found lineages and expand the control of their clan. The segmentary nature of the royal clan thus makes for a fluid and shifting relation among chiefs, and for shifting territorial control. The continued segmentation of a royal lineage and the proliferation of chiefs through this process results in a continuing expansion of the control of the lineage from which such segmentation takes place. The acknowledgment of the authority of a new chief by a group of commoners, whether this be by conquest or by peaceful invitation, means also their acknowledgment of the authority of the head of the lineage from which this new chief has segmented, and so on, up to the ruler as head of the whole royal lineage system.

The exclusive occupation of territory and rights over its disposition define the limits of a political entity, for one of the basic attributes of every state is territorial sovereignty.[1] It is clear that this is true of the Shambala state, for it might at any point in time be defined in terms of that territory within which the authority of the ruler was acknowledged. However, as Southall has pointed out, a segmentary lineage organization 'positively inhibits the rigid definition of territorial boundaries or of political powers, for the essence of it lies in a dynamic system of balance which renders such definition unnecessary or impossible. Recruitment is in terms of stable characteristics so that membership is permanent, yet the principle of unilineal descent, especially when localized, inherently predisposes to changes in the configuration of interrelationship of segments based upon it.'[2]

Shambalai as a Type of State

Although much has been written concerning the organization and character of the state, there has been a tendency to think in terms of the modern nation-state or to speak broadly of the

---

[1] R. M. MacIver, *The Modern State* (London: Oxford University Press, 1926), p. 22. ' . . . the state is an association . . . which maintains within a community territorially demarcated the universal external conditions of social order.'

[2] Aidan W. Southall, *Alur Society* (Cambridge: W. Heffer and Sons, 1956), p. 243.

characteristics of all states. A more refined handling of the problem of the characteristics of states has recently commanded interest. In anthropology this has taken the direction of tentative typologies such as that of Fortes and Evans-Pritchard and of detailed studies of systems which cannot be regarded as modern nations.[1] Such detailed studies preeminently have been the product of scholars specializing in African research, although Africanists certainly do not stand alone in what is a rapidly developing area of anthropology.[2]

There are certain characteristics which seem to be common to all states. Authorities from many different fields appear to agree that states may be distinguished from other political systems on the basis of the presence in them of a centralized authority, administrative machinery, and judicial institutions.[3]

In the modern nation the ongoing operation of the institutions of the state is facilitated by writing and further advances in the techniques of communication. The pre-literate community is at an extreme disadvantage in lacking the means of communication by which a large, dispersed population is unified and its activities coordinated. Redfield and others have pointed this up clearly in discussions of the folk society.[4] They view the non-literate society as characteristically small, isolated, homogeneous, and possessing a strong sense of group solidarity. Behavior is traditional, uncritical, and personal; there is no legislation, and the familial group is the unit of action. This is, of course, an ideal type and may be contrasted with an ideal type of modern urban society for analytic purposes. The tendency for certain characteristics to cluster is essential. In the absense of writing and means of rapid communication, com-

[1] Meyer Fortes and E. E. Evans-Pritchard, eds., *African Political Systems* (London: Oxford University Press, 1940).
[2] Recent highly significant studies in small-scale African states include: J. A. Barnes, *Politics in a Changing Society* (London: Oxford University Press, 1954), L. A. Fallers, *Bantu Bureaucracy* (Cambridge: W. Heffer and Sons, 1956), and Southall, *op. cit.*
[3] Cf. R. M. MacIver, *The Modern State* (London: Oxford University Press, 1926), p. 22; Meyer Fortes and E. E. Evans-Pritchard, eds., *op. cit.*, p. 5; Sir Henry Maine, *Ancient Law* (1st ed.; The World's Classics; London: Oxford University Press, 1931).
[4] Robert Redfield, 'The Folk Society', *The American Journal of Sociology*, LII (January, 1947), pp. 293–308.

Introduction

munities are often small, homogeneous face-to-face units within which unity may be readily maintained. The formation of larger social groupings must depend upon a heavy concentration on special means for channeling authority.[1] This has been increasingly recognized through the study of segmentary societies or those with age organization, secret societies, or other types of associations in which authority is legitimized and there is the provision of sanctions for the maintenance of the system. Such systems have come to be recognized as occupying a 'middle range' of complexity, with the development of institutions allowing the coordination of rather large aggregates.[2] Nevertheless they are nearly always homogeneous in language, culture, and tribal derivation.

The development of specialized institutions which allow the integration of relatively large heterogeneous populations may be taken to denote the upper range of social complexity. Very frequently in African states, and elsewhere as well, this takes the form of the clear separation of an elite from the rank and file. This elite is made recognizably distinct by various elaborate devices which focus attention upon it as a group.

The traditional history and the genealogies of the royal clan of the Shambala are together an account of the development of the state. Whether this account is historically accurate is of little importance to the people who relate it. What is important is that it acts as a charter. This charter specifically identifies the right to rule through the idea of the inheritance of special qualities by persons viewed as descendents of a hero. Further, it establishes an order of precedence in the hierarchy and in the succession to chiefships. It also provides guides for the proper behavior of ruler and ruled and indicates the limitations on the legitimate power of the rulers. Finally, it focuses and maintains attention upon the channels of communication which it provides.

Following Barnes and Southall, this system is here classed as a segmentary state.[3] The segmentary state is seen as a clear type within the category of states which differs importantly from

[1] Walter Goldschmidt, 'Social Organization in Native California and the Origin of Clans', *American Anthropologist*, Vol. 50, No. 3 (1948), p. 453.
[2] Meyer Fortes, 'The Structure of Unilineal Descent Groups', *American Anthropologist*, Vol. 55, No. 1 (1953), p. 24.
[3] J. A. Barnes, *op. cit.*; and A. W. Southall, *op. cit.*

other state types and at the same time cannot be grouped within the type of segmentary societies as set up by Fortes and Evans-Pritchard.[1]

[1] Meyer Fortes and E. E. Evans-Pritchard, eds., *op. cit.*, p. 5.

Chapter II

THE SETTING

THE Shambala today occupy nearly the whole of the Usambara Mountains of Northeastern Tanganyika, which lie between 4° 30′ S. and 5° 15′ S. Modern Shambala country is officially delimited by the boundaries of the Lushoto District of the Tanga Province; but the Shambala do not occupy the whole of this administrative district and the people themselves are not restricted to this region, for they are also found in the neighboring Districts of Pare on the northwest and Tanga on the southeast. The traditional extent of the country of Shambalai and the present extent of Shambala culture cannot be exactly determined. The Shambala were an expanding group, and their boundaries in the past were fluctuating and fluid. Beyond this, there are no sharp breaks in the cultures or languages of this region except where the high country gives way to the seemingly limitless stretches of the East African Plateaus which are occupied by pastoral Masai and Kwavi.

The Bantu-speaking Bondei, Zigua, and Nguu, who are situated to the southeast, speak languages that are mutually intelligible with each other and with Kishambala.[1] The Pare (or Asu), who occupy the mountain block northwest of the Usambaras, are also Bantu speakers, but the language is not so closely related and is not mutually intelligible with Kishambala. However, contact is very close between the two groups, and there are substantial numbers of Pare living in the Usambara Mountains.

On the north and south, the Shambala are bordered by

[1] Like other Bantu languages, those of Northeastern Tanganyika possess class prefixes. Thus the country is termed Usambara, the people Washambala (or Washambara, r and l not being significantly different in Kishambala), a person Mshambala. For the sake of simplicity, I shall here follow the accepted practice of omitting prefixes wherever possible. Since no standard orthography has been developed, Shambala words are written according to local spelling and no attempt is made in this study to develop a phonetically accurate orthography.

7

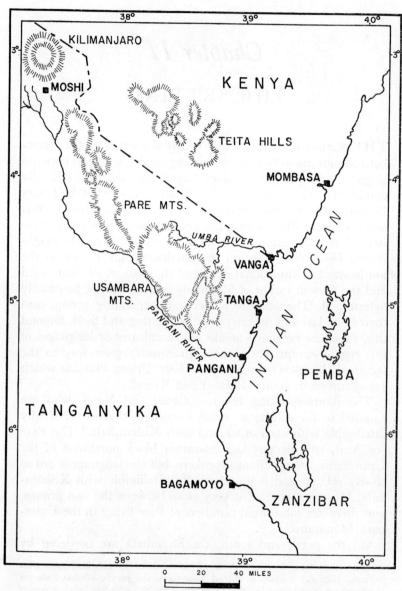

USAMBARA AND THE COAST

8

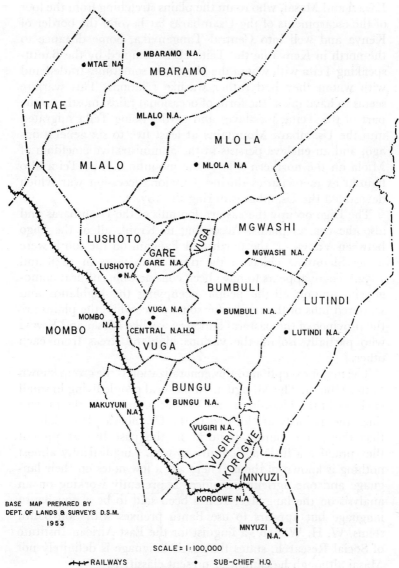

MBARAMO N.A.

MTAE NA

MBARAMO

MTAE

MLALO N.A.

MLOLA

MLALO

MLOLA N.A

MGWASHI

LUSHOTO

GARE

VUGA

MGWASHI N.A.

GARE N.A.

LUSHOTO
N.A.

BUMBULI

LUTINDI

VUGA N.A

BUMBULI N.A.

MOMBO
N.A.

MOMBO

CENTRAL N.A.H.Q.

LUTINDI N.A.

VUGA

BUNGU

BUNGU N.A.

MAKUYUNI
N.A.

VUGIRI N.A.

VUGIRI

KOROGWE

MNYUZI

KOROGWE N.A

BASE MAP PREPARED BY
DEPT. OF LANDS & SURVEYS D.S.M.
1953

MNYUZI
N.A.

SCALE = 1:100,000

RAILWAYS • SUB-CHIEF H.Q.
SUB-CHIEFDOM BOUNDARY DISTRICT BOUNDARY

CHIEFDOM OF SHAMBALAI

9

Kwavi and Masai, who roam the plains stretching from the foot of the escarpments of the Usambaras far beyond the border of Kenya and well into Central Tanganyika. Some distance to the north in Kenya lie the Teita Hills occupied by the Bantu-speaking Teita with whom the Shambala sometimes traded and with whom they had rather warlike relations. This warfare seems to have taken the form of occasional raids, mostly on the part of the Teita, for slaves and cattle. Some Teita migrated into the Usambara Mountains at least five to six generations ago, and an enclave persists in the administrative chiefdom of Mlola on the northern side of the mountains. The Teita also figured as mercenaries during a major succession war which devastated the Usambaras during the 1870's.

The Digo occupy the eastern foothills of the Usambaras and also the coastal plains. According to Krapf, all of the Digo between Vanga on the north and Pangani on the south were under Shambala chiefs at the time of his visits in 1848 and 1852.[1] There appears to have been considerable cultural homogeneity among all the people occupying the highlands and scattered hills of the region for some time, while the plains are the province of the pastoral and very warlike Masai and Kwavi who partially isolate the various highland areas from each other.

The major exception to this generalization is the group known as the Mbugu. The Mbugu are a pastoral people living in small enclaves in the Usambara and Pare Mountains. At the present time, the majority are located in the Usambaras. It is claimed that they were purely pastoral in the past but at present they practice a little agriculture as well. Linguistically almost nothing is known of them. There are a few notes on their language and one agriculture officer is presently working on an analysis on the language. It has been said to be a non-Bantu language but appears to use Bantu prefixes with non-Bantu stems. W. H. Whitely, a linguist for the East African Institute of Social Research, states that their language is definitely not Masai although he cannot at present classify it.[2]

There are a number of accounts of the derivation of the

---

[1] J. L. Krapf, *Travels and Missionary Labours in East Africa* (London: Trubner and Co., 1860).

[2] Personal communication.

Mbugu. Lord Hailey quotes a tradition which holds them to be
an offshoot of the Masai who migrated from the area of Laiki-
piya in Kenya and also mentions a second tradition that they
were chased into the mountains by the Masai.[1] The tradition
which I collected maintained that they migrated from north-
central Tanganyika to the Pare Mountains and from there to
the Usambaras.

The various enclaves of Mbugu have their own headmen and
settle their own disputes, but all of them acknowledge the
suzerainty of the Shambala royal chiefs and act as minor chiefs
within the administrative hierarchy of the present Native
Authority. Disputes involving Shambala and Mbugu are invariably referred to the local Shambala chief, and in the past the
Mbugu rendered tribute to the Shambala chiefs.

The Bantu-speaking peoples of this region all practice mixed
agriculture and herding similar to that of the Shambala. Boys'
and girls' initiation rites seem to be fairly uniform for the Zigua,
Nguu, Bondei, and Shambala.[2]

Although the borders of Shambalai have been fluid, the
Shambala are concentrated in the high country of the Usambara Mountains which form the heart of the Lushoto District.
The eastern foothills of the mountains rise about twenty-five
miles inland from the coast of the Indian Ocean directly behind
the port of Tanga. From there the mountains run roughly
northwest for a distance of some seventy-five miles, terminating
in the Mkomazi Valley, which separates them from the Pare
Mountains. The Usambara system is divided into three blocks
by deep valleys which run north and south. The most important of these is the Luengera Valley, which divides the East and
West Usambaras. The Mlinga-Magrotto ridge is further separated from the East Usambaras by the Sigi Valley.

The East Usambaras are lower and less precipitous than the
West, but the mountains rise steeply from the plains on all sides
and are bordered nearly everywhere by great escarpments so
that one quickly attains altitudes of from 2500 to 3000 feet when
climbing out of the plains. The greatest altitudes attained are in

[1] Lord W. M. H. Hailey, *Native Administration in the British African Territories*,
Part I. East Africa: Uganda, Kenya, Tanganyika (London: His Majesty's Stationery
Office, 1950), p. 327.
[2] H. Cory, *African Figurines* (New York: The Grove Press, 1956).

the west, where several peaks of around 7000 feet are found. The steep scarps and the deeply dissected nature of the uplands have very important effects upon the climate, which is relatively cool and stimulating everywhere in the mountains although extremely variable from place to place. Temperature is largely within the 60° to 80° range but drops somewhat lower in the highest zone and increases towards the coast. Annual rainfall figures have been recorded for some time in several parts of the mountains and surrounding plains and indicate variations from less than 10 inches on the plains to more than 80 inches in some parts of the mountains.[1] Most places receive between 40 and 50 inches of rainfall per year in two, or in some places three, rainy seasons.

The mountains as a whole were under rain forest in early times; and there still remain some extensive areas of forest, much of which is now preserved by the Forestry Department or the Native Authority in the form of forest reserves. Areas of cedar and tropical hardwoods have been commercially exploited for timber since the days of German administration. After generations of occupation, great areas have been cleared and are either under cultivation or grasses and low bush at the present time. The soils of most of the country are red to brown sandy loams broken by many outcrops of gneiss. There are thick rich soils in some of the stream valleys, but most of the country is hillside, where soil is thin and quickly exhausted or eroded away by continued cropping without rotation or fallowing. On the plains at the foot of the mountains the cover is largely grass and xerophytic bush with gray saline-alkaline soils. One agriculture officer suggested the soil picture might be summed up by viewing the mountains as a lump of rock surrounded by a sea of salt.

Economy and Demography

The Shambala are primarily arable cultivators relying on the hoe as their main agricultural implement, but they also keep cattle and small stock in significant numbers which they graze

---

[1] *Summary of Rainfall for the Year 1955, Part II, Tanganyika* (Nairobi: East African Meteorological Department, 1955). These figures are from scattered stations and by no means represent the degree of local variation in broken uplands of this nature. Such variation, of course, has a great effect upon local cultivation.

in unopened bush, commonage near the villages, and harvested fields.[1] The main crops in order of importance are maize, beans, cassava, sweet potatoes, bananas, and sugar cane. In addition to these crops, wattle bark, vegetables, coffee, rice, cotton, and tobacco are grown for the market, and small amounts of other crops are produced. Production for the market is becoming increasingly important and is encouraged by the administration.

The diet upon which the Shambala rely is predominately starchy, composed as it is of maize or cassava porridge varied by beans, bananas or sweet potatoes. Some green vegetables are added as a relish, and those people who keep cattle get some milk, which is usually soured and eaten in the morning with left-overs from the previous night. Local authorities are of the opinion that the consumption of meat is increasing, but stock is primarily used for other purposes than food. Cattle and small stock figure prominently in bride wealth and ceremonial, but are also of vast importance in patterns of clientship. One of the most important ways in which a man can increase his power and prestige is through stock lending. By lending stock to others it is possible to build up a widely ramifying network of supporters who can be called upon for aid in legal difficulties or bad times. Chiefs depend to a considerable extent upon stock lending as a means of binding their followers to them, while clients in turn find the relation beneficial, for they are allowed to keep the milk from these animals and are given a proportion of the offspring with which they may start their own herds.[2] A proverb sums up Shambala stock practices neatly: 'They who live with the cattle are not the rich, but the poor.'

Although maize and cassava are now the mainstays of the diet, this has not always been the case. Many older people can recall a time when little or no cassava was cultivated. It has been promoted as a drought crop and is easy to grow, so that it is now very popular. Johanssen and Döring, writing in 1915, seem to indicate that bananas were then planted more extensively

---

[1] Stock census taken in 1952 indicated a total of 88,658 cattle and 88,727 small stock (mostly sheep and goats), giving a grand total of 177,385 animals. Of this total 97,742 were in the mountains and 79,643 were on the plains.

[2] The proportion of animals a client may keep varies according to the animals being herded and the region of the mountains. In many places no cattle may be retained but every fourth goat or sheep born belongs to the herder. A few generous men occasionally give a bull calf to their herder.

than they are at the present time.[1] Many older informants corroborate this impression and proverbs appear to support it as well. Evidently bananas have gradually been replaced by increasing amounts of maize and cassava, which the people prefer. Government is now attempting to increase banana planting since it is not as hard on the soil as is maize and provides more protection against erosion on steep slopes.

The mixed farming and herding economy supports a very dense population in the mountains. Villages are close together and nearly all of the available land is under cultivation. Overpopulation is an extremely grave problem with which the administration must deal, for it means continual cropping with no chance to rest the soil through fallowing. This has led to a very rapid deterioration of the soil and lowered yields, a problem which can only be met by even more frequent cropping. This state of affairs has prompted the institution of corrective measures in the form of a planned program called the Usambara Development Scheme. This scheme, which is now in operation, was preceded by a pilot study in the Mlalo Basin, which is one of the most heavily populated parts of the mountains. Detailed studies which were undertaken during this project indicated a population density per square mile of cultivated land of 995 persons, with a density for the whole basin, including land too steep to utilize, of 461 persons per square mile.[2] Densities here are undoubtedly higher than in many parts of the mountains and plains, for the total population of the District was reported as 219,152 for an area of 4,241 square miles in 1948.[3] These figures give no indication of actual densities, however, for they include much plains land occupied by small groups of Masai and Kwavi, large tracts of forest reserve and game reserve, land alienated to Europeans, and land too steep to cultivate. District agricultural officers estimate that at least 1890 square miles of the District are unsuitable for agricultural

---

[1] E. Johanssen, and P. Döring, 'Das Leben der Schambala', *Zeitschrift für Kolonialsprachen*, Band V (Berlin: Dietrich Reimer, 1915), p. 7. The authors here state, 'Das Land ist, soweit es bewohnt ist, mit Bananenbeständen bedeckt, zwischen denen Mais-, Zucherrohr-, und Bohnenfelder sich hinstrecken.'

[2] *Report of the Mlalo Rehabilitation Scheme*, October, 1949, document on file at the District Office, Lushoto, Tanga Province.

[3] 'African Population of Tanganyika Territory', *Geographical and Tribal Studies* (*Source: East African Population Census, 1948*) (Nairobi: East African Statistical Department, 1950), p. 71.

purposes. Further, the crude figures of the 1957 census which are now available indicate a fairly rapid rate of population increase. Total population at the time of this second census was 263,887 or 44,735 higher than 1948. The rate of increase calculated by the geometric method for the district is then 1·20% per annum.

It appears likely that the problems of soil exhaustion and serious erosion are relatively recent and are the result of increasing population and the stability imposed by European administration. In former times the Shambala expanded their domains through the processes of lineage segmentation and warfare. Such expansion was probably partially internal through the clearing of new land but also occurred at the expense of surrounding peoples less highly organized than the Shambala. At present the cessation of warfare and the introduction of western medicine have probably lowered the mortality rate while simultaneously migration has been reduced. These factors seem likely to have hastened the problems of pressure on the land which now confront the area. Judgments such as this are extremely tenuous, however, for the early population estimates are poor at best and little trust can be put in figures projected into the past. The inaccuracy of estimated figures can be best appreciated by a comparison of the last territorial estimate with the figures of the census of 1948. The 1947 estimate gave the population of Tanganyika as 5,838,000, while the 1948 Census revealed the population to be 7,408,000.[1]

It seems certain, however, that the population of the Usambaras has been expanding. This process of expansion has not been solely through natural increase but has also been the result of immigration. The ethnic composition of Shambalai is quite heterogeneous. Not only is the Usambara Highland more suitable for agriculture than the surrounding plains, but it is also relatively free of malaria. In addition, the rapid expansion of the political domination of the Shambala has brought many groups of differing tribal origin under their control and added to the diversity. The problems of the recruitment of new people will be taken up at some length when the nature of the Shambala political system is examined. Suffice it

---

[1] East African Statistical Department, *Quarterly Economic and Statistical Bulletin*, June, 1952 (revised 1948 Census figures).

to say here that the most outstanding feature of the system is the extension of the rule of the royal clan, which added to its power by the continual addition of new subjects. Such expansion took place within the Usambara Mountains and also spread over other groups in the vicinity. At the same time, it appears that new migrants were constantly welcomed into the mountains and settled under one or another chief. The only condition for such settlement appears to have been willingness to accept the culture and values of the royal clan. The diverse origin of the modern Shambala is considered by them to be of great importance, and appears to the observer to have a double-edged significance. On the one hand, the majority of people will identify themselves immediately as Shambala, but I was never able to find an informant who would not qualify this after some reflection by adding that really his ancestors came to the Usambara Mountains from elsewhere. I did not encounter a single oral tradition that traced an origin within the present limits of Shambala political control or suggested that some group was the original Shambala. Everyone is, in the final analysis, an immigrant. On the other hand, most modern residents share a common culture, speak a common language, and owe allegiance to the paramount chief. Their oral traditions and genealogies recount how this came about and are held to explain how they regard themselves as Shambala and why others regard them as such.

There are distinctions, however, which are based upon the length of time over which people have resided within the Usambara Mountains. Immigration into this region has been a continuous process which has endured over a long period and which still continues today, although it has diminished to a trickle because of the stability imposed by British administration, and the present shortage of land. The immediate response of individuals who themselves have moved into the Usambaras or whose fathers or grandfathers immigrated is to identify themselves according to their tribe of origin while others generally call themselves Shambala. These distinctions appear clearly in census data for the Lushoto District. The East African census of 1948 lists the main tribes of the Lushoto District in order of importance as the Shambala (listed as Sambaa, the government spelling), Nguu, Zigua (Zighula), Pare (Asu),

Mbugu, Nyamwezi, and Bondei. In addition to these, 13 per cent of the District total is made up of a congeries of individuals of other tribal origins.[1] A good deal of this heterogeneity exists on the plains surrounding the mountains. Here are located the large sisal plantations which attract workers from all over Tanganyika, and here also lie territories held by some of these other tribes. Nevertheless, the census reveals that even within the mountain regions, places which attract relatively little large-scale labor migration, there are substantial numbers of people who do not call themselves Shambala. In no region of the mountains does the proportion of people identified as Shambala exceed 80 per cent. These census data do not by any means reveal the true heterogeneity of the population, however, for, as I have said, even those who identify themselves as Shambala retain a view of themselves as ultimately being immigrants. What the census figures reveal is a complex set of attitudes about tribal identification. Early migrants are likely to call themselves Shambala, while those who have arrived within the last two generations or who came as members of large, strongly integrated groups are likely to identify themselves by their place of origin. Further, those near the borders who have constant contact with people not under the domination of the royal clan of the Shambala are less likely to identify themselves as Shambala.

Political boundaries may be relatively sharp, but in an expanding state they are fluid and shifting; beyond this, it is seldom that the limits of a culture and a social system exactly coincide. As Fortes has pointed out: 'A culture, certainly in most of Africa, and I venture to believe in many other areas too . . . has no clear-cut boundaries. But a group of people bound together within a single social structure have a boundary, though not necessarily one that coincides with a physical boundary or is impenetrable.'[2]

[1] 'African Population of Tanganyika Territory', *Geographical and Tribal Studies* (Nairobi: East African Statistical Department, 1950), pp. 71-3. This material is based on the 1948 census. A new ten-year census was taken in 1957 but the results are not yet available in full detail.
[2] Meyer Fortes, 'The Structure of Unilineal Descent Groups', *American Anthropologist*, Vol. 55, No. 1 (1953), p. 22.

Historical Background

It is in this expansive form that our historical knowledge of the Shambala system begins. Written records of Shambalai start at a time when the state was large and growing larger. Of the factors which set the process in motion, or of the events of its formation, we have no direct evidence but only the testimony of oral tradition. However, the early missionary and explorer, J. L. Krapf, twice visited the Usambara Mountains in the course of his explorations and has left a very useful account of his observations.[1]

Krapf's first visit was in 1848, when he decided to proceed overland to the Usambaras from his base near Mombasa. This decision was prompted by what he had heard from the people of the coast about Kimweri, king of Usambara. He records that he passed the borders of Shambalai on July 24, 1848, and that by July 28 was intercepted by a message from the king inviting him to proceed to the capital of the kingdom at Vuga. It took Krapf himself nine more days to get to Vuga, which is some indication of the communications and control existing within Shambalai at that time. Kimweri was extremely friendly and receptive to Krapf's desire to establish missions and expressed an interest in having teachers and a medical man sent to the Usambaras. Krapf's first visit was quite short, for, once assured of a friendly welcome, he wished to return quickly to Mombasa.

Although Kimweri had pressed him for the promise of a return in three or four months, Krapf did not attempt a second journey to the Usambaras until 1852. During the course of his two visits Krapf had considerable opportunity to observe the workings of the Shambala state and was much impressed by it, being moved to a long aside in his book about the superiority of monarchy over democracy. During both of his trips he was guided by representatives from the capital and was lodged at public expense in the villages along the way. At Vuga he was put up in a house meant for guests and was waited on by a royal functionary called Mbereko, who brought him a sheep and other provisions. None of the village chiefs begged for gifts, and he was told the king would not allow it. He found the region

[1] J. L. Krapf, *Travels and Missionary Labours in East Africa* (London: Trubner & Co., 1860).

divided into 'districts' under 'governors' who were the sons and daughters of the king and was told that each 'governor' was required to have at the capital a representative, called Mlau, through whom all state business was transacted. Of the functionaries at the capital, he has relatively little to say, mentioning only three: Mdoe whom he identifies as the Vizier; Mboki, or army commander; and Mbereko, or captain of the king's bodyguard.[1]

Krapf records that Kimweri ruled over an area approximately 60 miles wide from north to south, and 140 miles wide east to west, which Krapf estimated to contain approximately half a million people. The southern boundary seems to have been the Pangani River; to the north, Kimweri controlled the course of the Umba River and the Indian Ocean formed his eastern boundary. Of Kimweri's claim to the coast there seems to be little doubt, for Krapf's affirmation is supported by an earlier account of 1853 cited by Coupland.[2]

The Shambala state was probably relatively young at the time of Krapf's visits. Kimweri's claims on the coast appear to have been of no great antiquity, for they were adjusted between Kimweri and Seyyid Said, who was Sultan of Zanzibar from 1806 to 1856. Said had acquired claims to the coast between Mombasa and Pangani from the Arab Mazrui dynasty of Mombasa in 1837 but acknowledged the rights of Kimweri to everything but the towns of Tanga and Pangani.[3] Said reserved the right to appoint governors at Tanga and Pangani, which were old established ports in the Arab trade network, but he arrived at a compromise with Kimweri in that Kimweri appointed his own headmen (called *Diwans* in the Arab style) everywhere else. That Said retained some interest in the region is demonstrated by the fact that he also recognized the *Diwans* appointed by Kimweri and gave them gifts at their appointment. This arrangement appears to have been the product of negotiation between Kimweri and Said and may not have prevailed before Kimweri's time. Thus, the addition of the

[1] J. L. Krapf, *op. cit.*, pp. 272–5, 369–405.
[2] R. Coupland, *East Africa and Its Invaders* (London: Oxford University Press, 1938), p. 352. Coupland cites W. H. Sykes, *Journal of the Royal Geography Society*, XXIII (1853), to the effect that Kimweri held the coast between the Island of Wasin on the north and the Pangani River on the south (4° 30′ S. to 5° 30′ S.).
[3] R. Coupland, *op. cit.*, p. 351.

coast to Shambalai could have taken place little before 1837, for it was in that year that the Mazrui claims to the coast passed to Said Seyyid, Sultan of Zanzibar.[1]

The Arabs must have been well acquainted with the kingdom of Usambara; it impinged on their claims to the coast and, in addition, one of the important caravan routes to the interior passed through it. The major route to the interior was located to the south with its coastal terminal at Bagamoyo opposite Zanzibar. However, Pangani, from which the valley of the Pangani River penetrates all the way to the slopes of Mount Kilimanjaro, was an important point of export for slaves.[2] Considerable amounts of ivory were also shipped from Tanga and Pangani, and Kimweri claimed a monopoly within his boundaries on the trade in slaves and ivory.[3] It is tempting to speculate about the role of the ivory and slave trades in the formation of the Shambala state, but I have not found sufficient documentation to advance such a thesis.

The traditional history of the Shambala does not claim any great antiquity for the state. It is recounted partly in the form of a genealogy which lists only three rulers before Kimweri, and it is quite specific in recounting how each of these rulers expanded his control by dispatching his sons to surrounding villages. If one puts any trust in such oral traditions, the area controlled by Kimweri was much larger than that controlled by any of his predecessors. Kimweri was an elderly man at the time of Krapf's visits and Baumann places his death in 1869.[4] He probably could not have been born much before 1800. Assigning approximately twenty years to each generation, this would put the formation of the state at around 1740. For the time being, the factors bringing about its formation and the duration of its existence must remain in the realm of guesswork. It is nevertheless quite certain that Arab influences were of some importance, as evidenced by Said's treaty with Kimweri, and Krapf's observation of numbers of Swahili and Arabs at the capital. Indeed, an Arab from Zanzibar was Kimweri's personal physician at the time of Krapf's visits. Further, it is quite clear

[1] R. Coupland. *op. cit.*, p. 292.
[2] J. L. Krapf, *op. cit.*, p. 373. [3] *Ibid.*, p. 373.
[4] O. Baumann, *Usambara und seine Nachbargebiete* (Berlin: Dietrich Reimer, 1891), p. 186.

that the trade route passing up the Pangani was important to
the Arabs. Said even erected a fort within Kimweri's domains
near Mt. Tongwe' to keep the route open when Kimweri had
trouble with the Zigua to the south.[1]

Major Features of Kinship and Political Structure

The Shambala are a patrilineal people practising predominately virilocal residence. The people live in close settlements
which have the nature of lineage-villages. Most small villages
are predominately occupied by males of only one lineage with
a few men related by marriage or attached by filiation. Larger
villages usually contain more than one lineage, in which case
the lineage which is senior in occupancy is dominant. The villages of royal chiefs tend to be more heterogeneous, containing besides the chiefly lineage perhaps several attached minor
lineages and many men bound to the chief through cattle-
clientship and other means. The localized lineage is a corporate
group which holds land, has a recognized leader who is a senior
male member and is *primus inter pares* in a council of all adult
lineage members, conducts its own ceremonies of ancestor worship, and is regarded as a unit by all others.

The localized lineages are associated into dispersed patrilineal clans which are named and, to a certain extent, ranked.
The lineage, however, is generally the largest unit which acts as
a body. Most clans possess no leadership and no machinery for
joint action. The clan cannot be considered to hold land, rather
land is held by the constituent lineages of which the clan is
composed. The observance of exogamy and the possession of a
name, a vague feeling of membership, and a few traditions of
origin seem to be the major elements shared by the lineages of
which most clans are composed. Such clans are very numerous
in Shambalai; I counted over forty, and it is certain that there
are more than this number. Some clans are very large, with
lineages located in all sections of the country; some are small
and may be composed of no more than two or three lineages.

---

[1] Burton and Speke passed through the Usambaras on their trip of exploration
to Lake Victoria and spent one day with Kimweri at Vuga in 1857. Speke observed
Said's fort garrisoned with 25 Baluchis, 'on a hill called Tongwe, near the Pangani
River . . .' J. H. Speke, *What Led to the Discovery of the Source of the Nile* (London:
William Blackwood, 1864), p. 174.

At least two clans depart from this general pattern, being composed of deep segmentary systems in which the lineages are articulated one to another in terms of long and elaborate genealogies. Within clans of this type, relations at one level are defined in terms of solidarity at a higher level of segmentation. The unit which emerges depends upon the activities at hand and may be much larger than the localized segment inhabiting a single village. Thus, such clans possess a potentiality for organization far greater than that which is characteristic of the majority of Shambala clans. The outstanding example of a clan of this sort is the royal Wakilindi clan.

In the structure of Shambala society, the principle of ascribed rank places this clan above all others. By birth, members are assigned a higher status and an inborn fitness to rule. Rulership is a core feature of Shambala society which distinguishes it from all of the surrounding groups with which it shares so much linguistically and culturally.

Most of the tribes of the region are organized into small independent chiefdoms which are today united by Government into federations for the purposes of territorial administration. If tradition is to be trusted, this was the pattern also followed in the Usambara Mountains. At least three generations before modern European contact migrants from Zigua country instituted a process, to be examined in some detail later, which ultimately expanded into domination of the existing population. Whether or not changes in political organization began exactly in this way makes little difference at the present time, for this tradition is firmly believed by the Shambala and forms part of the charter (in the Malinowskian sense)[1] for the present Shambala state. It is clear that in the later stages of the state, the domination of the royal clan of the Shambala was in a process of expansion. This expansion was the product of at least two intimately connected processes. On the one hand, there was domination

---

[1] B. Malinowski, 'Myth in Primitive Psychology', in *Magic, Science and Religion and Other Essays* (New York: Doubleday and Company, 1955), p. 101. Malinowski here advances the view that, 'Myth fulfills in primitive culture an indispensable function: it expresses, enhances, and codifies belief; it safeguards and enforces morality; it vouches for the efficiency of ritual and contains practical rules for the guidance of man. Myth is thus a vital ingredient of human civilization; it is not an idle tale, but a hard-worked active force; it is not an intellectual explanation or an artistic imagery, but a pragmatic charter of primitive faith and moral wisdom.'

through force of arms and planned campaigns. On the other hand, the continued segmentation of the royal lineage led to the establishment of new chiefs derived from the lineages of old chiefs. These new chiefs administered a section of the territory of the old chief or peacefully added to the domains of the old chief by being invited to reside along the previous borders of these domains by the indigenous occupants. The greater part of the expansion of the Shambala state appears to have been of the latter type, and I will attempt to show that this was an expression of tensions internal to the system. Even that planned extension of domination which resulted from warfare appears to have been largely in response to the segmentary tendencies within royal lineages.

Like the lineages of other clans, the Wakilindi lineages have a corporate structure of authority, and corporate economic and religious interests; but, unlike commoner lineages, the unit of reference in these elements extends downward to embrace the whole of the clan and outward to the state as a whole. In theory, all of the people and all of the things within Shambalai are the property of the ruler. Anyone who comes to live within Shambalai has to acknowledge the authority of the ruler. The Shambala may be defined as that group of people which owes allegiance to a common ruler called the *Simbamwene*. These people combined under the ruler to attack or defend themselves against outside groups. In addition to his role in external relations, the ruler exercises judicial, administrative, and legislative authority over his people, with power to enforce his decisions. He also performs religious ceremonies and magical acts on behalf of his people.

The authority of the ruler as representative of the royal clan extends over the members of all clans to the state as a whole. His interests are national interests, his ancestors, national ancestors, his rituals, public ceremonies. Crimes are viewed as injuries to him and part of every fine is his due. The royal clan is then more than *primus inter pares* among clans; it is the symbolic embodiment of the unity of the state, and its structure imparts a structure to the state. Thus the royal clan controls not only the rulership, but also most of the subordinate chiefships above that of the leader of the commoner lineage-village.

The final links in the hierarchy of authority are the heads

23

of commouer lineages. These men are directly under the lesser royal chiefs and form the broad base of the political organization. The position of the commoner lineage head is of a different quality than that of any royal chief. Such a lineage head is the moral and jural representative of his lineage and exercises a measure of familial authority within this group, but his authority does not extend beyond his own lineage. Unless a lineage head is acting under a royal command, he does not have much coercive power, but rather leads discussions and gains decisions through the deference paid to senior men and the habits of cooperation within the lineage.

Post-Contact Modifications

The general outlines of the system have been maintained despite the considerable rearrangements following Krapf's pioneering visits. Krapf himself asked for and obtained Kimweri's permission to erect a mission in Shambalai and in 1853 Erhardt, one of Krapf's associates in the Church Missionary Society, established a mission on Mount Tongwe' on land designated by Kimweri. This mission has had a varied history; Erhardt had to leave after only a few months because of poor health, but it has been revived intermittently. Following upon these efforts of Krapf and his associates, there were other explorations into the interior which passed through Shambalai. Burton and Speke, Von der Decken, Allington, and others visited the region. Allington established a Universities' Mission to Central Africa (U.M.C.A.) in Kimweri's territory at Magila in 1868 which operated briefly and then closed until 1875, when it was reopened. This mission is still active today despite the interruptions of wars and other difficulties.

The Germans quickly appreciated the agricultural possibilities of the Northern Highlands of their colony and in 1890, Baumann, a geographer, was commissioned by the Deutschostafrikanischen Gesellschaft to survey and map the Usambaras and their surroundings.[1] This project was of primary importance, for the German administration not only considered the Usambaras, Pares, Kilimanjaro, and Arusha as their best agricultural lands but also were looking toward a railway to

[1] O. Baumann, *op. cit.*

link Lake Victoria to the port of Tanga, which they preferred
to Dar es Salaam.[1] Baumann not only mapped and collected
specimens, but also gives a fairly detailed description of events
as he found them in 1890. His picture of the Shambala state
agrees well with that of Krapf, and there is a good discussion of
the events which led to a succession war following the death of
Kimweri in 1869.

This struggle was extremely bitter and protracted and led
to considerable changes in the state. Although it started as a
contest over who should succeed within the existing structure,
grave splits soon occurred among the various great chiefs and
major portions of the state broke away. These various chiefs
sought allies outside Shambalai and thus became quickly involved in the issues of the partitioning of Africa. Thus one
faction allied itself with Mbaruk bin Rashid, the last of the
Mazrui dynasty of Mombasa. This immediately brought the
Sultan of Zanzibar into the conflict since he was forced by this
to recognize the other major faction which then carried his flag
until the inception of German rule. The German East Africa
Company was briefly allied with Mbaruk and so was drawn in
also. In addition, the Zigua, Teita, Masai, and Chagga were
solicited as allies by one or another chief. Finally the German
government entered the dispute and in 1890 established a fort
on the plains at Masinde in order to stabilize the caravan route
and stop raids.[2]

After this act, the Germans recognized as paramount Semboja, a son of Kimweri then chief at Masinde, and awarded him
a salary. This did little to quiet the trouble, however, for much
of the population regarded this chief as a usurper since he was
younger than other sons of Kimweri, and since Kimweri had
favored another who had been duly installed. Baumann has to
say of this man:

> Not long after Kimeri's death the cunning Semboja gathered
> around him a robber gang of Wazigua, coastal people and others
> and with these unexpectedly attacked Vuga, succeeded in over-
> coming Shekulavu (then paramount) and driving him to Bum-
> buli. The latter gathered his power there and would probably
> have driven the usurper out of Vuga again, if death had not struck

[1] W. Fitzgerald, *Africa* (7th rev. edn., London: Methuen and Co., 1950), p. 231.
[2] O. Baumann, *op. cit.*, p. 186 *passim*.

him during the preparations. He left behind, as his first born, a minor son Kinyassi, who was looked upon, and still is, as rightful chief of Vuga in Usambara in general. In absence of a proper chief it is understandable that there was never any general installation.[1]

This succession war will be discussed in a later chapter at which time the importance of a general installation will be assessed. Here it is of importance in that lack of proper recognition by the competent authorities continued to plague Semboja and thus indirectly the German administration which had recognized him. The resistance offered to Semboja had earlier prompted him to install his son Kimweri as ruler. This did little to settle the difficulties, for there had still been no regular installation. Thus when Semboja's son, Kimweri, died in 1870, Semboja placed his second son, Mputa, in the capital,[2] and it was really he, rather than Semboja, whom the Germans should have recognized although he was subject to the same claims of improper installation as Semboja. The struggle over the paramountcy became so intense that the Germans deposed Mputa in 1895 and hanged him for murder. They then temporarily appointed Kibanga, a great chief, as regent until the claimant supported by the faction opposed to Semboja and his lineage could be properly installed.

Thus it was that in late 1985 Kinyasi, great grandson of Kimweri in the senior lineage derived from Kimweri, became the ruler. By then the Germans were thoroughly discouraged in their attempt to rule through the indigenous system and so brought in *Akidas* (political agents from the coast) to accompany each royal chief in the pattern they had adopted elsewhere, following the style of the Sultan of Zanzibar. Kinyasi was retained until 1903, when he abdicated through fear of assassination. The state had been nearly destroyed by the prolonged fighting and the external intervention. The *Akida* system was the main bulwark of German rule in the years after 1902, and it is reported that in 1903 an *Akida* named Ngoma ran the area from the town of Korogwe on the Plains.[3]

[1] O. Baumann, *op. cit.*, p. 188 (my translation of the German).

[2] Officer in Charge, Masinde, to Reichscommissar, Dar es Salaam, 1895. On file at the District Office, Lushoto.

[3] 'History of the District' (Lushoto: District Book, Office of the District Commissioner).

1. The southern escarpment of the western Usambara Mountains as viewed from the plains. The face of the escarpment is quite sheer and only a few passes allow easy access to the uplands.

2. The Mlalo basin as seen from the southwest. The whole of the basin is under intense cultivation and is dotted with compact settlements around which the maize fields are oriented. Planting had just been completed at the time of this photo; note the very small proportion of land in fallow.

3. Intensive cultivation of green vegetables is carried out in stream bottoms. The tie-ridging is part of a Government scheme to increase yields and retard erosion.

Regardless of these upsets the Germans proceeded with their development of the area. They laid out the line for a railway, built a town below the mountains at Masinde, started rubber and coffee plantations, and began exploiting the cedar forests.[1] The railway was completed to Mombo, near Masinde, in 1905, but the aim of taking it to Lake Victoria had been abandoned by then in favor of a route through Central Tanganyika, and it was continued only as far as Moshi on the slopes of Mt. Kilimanjaro.[2] Paasche records that by 1906, Wilhelmstal, the present District Headquarters of Lushoto, was a flourishing center for German coffee plantations and the point where crops were assembled for shipment to the railway at Mombo.[3]

The Usambaras loomed large in German plans throughout their administration. The Amani Institute for tropical research was placed by them in the Eastern Usambaras; rubber and cinchona plantations were begun; sisal planting was introduced after the failure of the world rubber market just before World War I; and hospitals and resorts were projected since the climate provided a relief from the tropical conditions of the coast. Wilhelmstal even served briefly as the summer capital for the colony. The cinchona plantations were the principal source of quinine for the German troops during the 1914–18 war, and a major army camp was located in the mountains until capture by the British in 1916.[4]

This was a period of great impact upon the Shambala, who were made even more vulnerable by the succession difficulties which have been outlined. Not only did European administration alter the traditional system but planters and traders settled in the mountains. Beyond this, the U.M.C.A. and C.M.S. missions were very active in the western part of the region and the Bethel Lutheran Mission made great headway in the north, first in the regions of Mlalo, Mbaramo, and Mtae, and only slightly later in Vuga and elsewhere. This first impact had hardly been absorbed when World War I began and significant numbers of Shambala were enlisted in the German army. Even

---

[1] W. Fitzgerald, *op. cit.*, pp. 232–3.

[2] C. W. Leverett, 'An Outline of the History of Railways in Tanganyika 1890–1956', *Tanganyika Notes and Records*, Nos. 47 and 48 (1957).

[3] H. Paasche, *Deutsch-Ostafrika*, Berlin, 1906, p. 210 *passim*.

[4] M. Taute, 'A German Account of the Medical side of the War in East Africa, 1914–1918', *Tanganyika Notes and Records*, No. 8 (1939), p. 1.

those who did not fight were deeply involved because of the strategic and economic importance of the Usambara Mountains. This situation was again changed in two years by British capture of the mountains and the resulting change in administration.

The change of administrating powers was to bring many alterations, but these were slow in coming. The immediate changes were largely in the form of internment of the German planters and a temporary closing of the Bethel Mission which had been staffed by Germans. Administration continued under the authorities that had been recognized by the Germans until 1926 when Kinyasi, the last ruler who had abdicated under the Germans, was induced to return to office. This was an outgrowth of the policies of Sir Donald Cameron, then Governor of Tanganyika, who later wrote, with regard to the use of *Akidas*: 'It is curious that after the War when a Civil Administration was set up the British, too, failed to realize for several years how anomalous and bad the system was, continuing its use until Indirect Administration was set up in 1925 and the years following to replace it.'[1] The policies of Sir Donald were greeted enthusiastically by the Shambala according to a report of 1927. 'In Usambara the chiefdom known to early explorers as the important Kingdom of Vuga has been restored after an abeyance of some forty or fifty years, and so popular was this measure that a portion of the tribe living in Tanga District insisted on their inclusion in the Native Administration.'[2] In this manner the British began an attempt to govern through indigenous institutions which had been partially shattered but which still retained considerable vitality. The lapse of time alluded to in the above quotation is greatly exaggerated, no more than twenty-five years having passed since Kinyasi's abdication. Furthermore, the lower levels of royal chiefs had continued to function throughout. Thus the problem was not to recreate a completely defunct system but rather to resuscitate a rather badly mauled victim.

Unfortunately Kinyasi proved a poor choice for the resuscitation. The succession difficulties of German days had never been

---

[1] Sir Donald Cameron, 'Native Administration in Nigeria and Tanganyika', *Journal of the Royal African Society*, Vol. 36 (1937), p. 4.

[2] *Report to the Council of the League of Nations on the Administration of Tanganyika Territory for 1927* (London: His Majesty's Stationery Office, 1928), p. 98.

completely resolved but only smothered. Kinyasi met opposition from the descendants of Semboja's lineage and retreated to inactivity. He seems to have been timid and still suffering from the fears which led to his earlier abdication. After approximately three years in office he again resigned and stated that he wished his son, Mchami, as successor. However, the Administration decided the great chiefs should designate a ruler and in February, 1929, Billa Kimweri, son of Kimweri, grandson of Semboja, was elected. Billa died in August of the same year and there were charges of witchcraft and poisoning, but no evidence has ever been forthcoming.[1] Billa was succeeded by his brother Magogo, then Zumbe Mkuu of Mombo, who ruled until 1947, when he resigned in the face of considerable political agitation and was succeeded by his son Mputa, the present paramount chief. The rather complex order of succession may be seen on the accompanying chart.

On the surface, local government appears remarkably stable under British administration. There have been only four paramount chiefs in thirty-two years, two of whom together ruled only a total of approximately three years, the rest of the period being taken up by the two who have followed. In these terms the German administration comes off rather badly by comparison, but all of the troubles which plagued them and which culminated in hanging the paramount and instituting *Akidas* cannot be laid at their door. They undoubtedly arrived in the midst of great unrest which their presence would have aggravated regardless of the course they had chosen to take. Furthermore, the relative independence of action allowed the brothers and uncles of the ruler within the Shambala system probably would have caused them difficulty even had there been no violent expression of it when they arrived.

It appears likely that the abolition of the paramountcy and its subsequent reinstatement has made the ruler even more obviously dependent upon the sanctions of external law and external recognition than is usually the case in instances of Indirect Rule. This has had the effect of weakening his authority through partial undermining of the ritual and supernatural sanctions which existed in the old system, but at the same time

[1] *Annual Reports of the Provincial Commissioners on Native Administration for the year 1929* (Dar es Salaam: Government Printer, 1930), pp. 18–19.

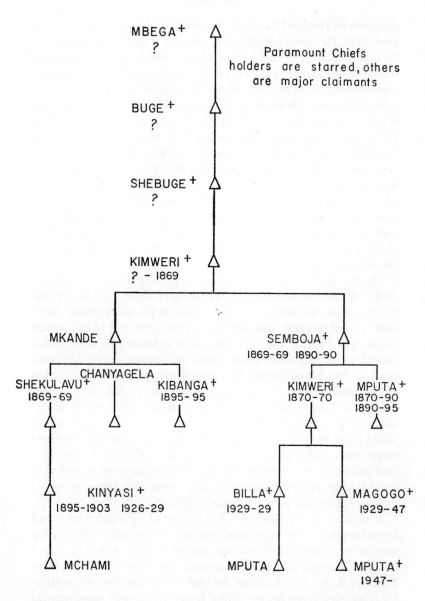

MBEGA +
?

Paramount Chiefs
holders are starred, others
are major claimants

BUGE +
?

SHEBUGE +
?

KIMWERI +
? - 1869

MKANDE

SEMBOJA +
1869-69 1890-90

CHANYAGELA

SHEKULAVU +
1869-69

KIBANGA +
1895-95

KIMWERI +
1870-70

MPUTA +
1870-90
1890-95

KINYASI +
1895-1903 1926-29

BILLA +
1929-29

MAGOGO +
1929-47

MCHAMI

MPUTA

MPUTA +
1947-

SUCCESSION TO SHAMBALA PARAMOUNTCY

it has reinforced his position vis-à-vis the great chiefs since it is clear that his authority over them is not simply a matter of lineage position. Resistance to the paramount and the pursuit of independent courses of action are, *ipso facto*, actions against the British government in a manner which never could have been the case during the period of German administration. Thus there has been little direct opposition to the paramount until recent years. Even today, in a period of mounting nationalism in Tanganyika, much of the opposition is covert. Twice since World War II there have been attempts to form local political parties, but neither effort has been sanctioned by the Administration and both have lapsed into underground movements. Most of the present opposition takes the form of word-of-mouth criticism, outward agreement with government policies but passive resistance to their implementation, secret meetings, and general inaction. Interpretations of this resistance as opposition to the "feudal" nature of the state seem partially misread, and although the introduction of the democratic process in the form of elective councils and an alteration of the Native Authority from Chief to Chief in Council is laudable, it does not answer what appears to me to be the major dissatisfaction. It is not opposition to the royal clan *per se*, or to the traditional chiefs, which motivates political agitation but rather opposition to the Administration operating through them and to the particular lineage which now holds the paramountcy. The present paramount is seen by many Shambala as a direct agent of the Government of Tanganyika and activities against him are in fact attempts to gain a greater voice and assert other values vis-à-vis the Government, not vis-à-vis the royal clan.

Such considerations aside, there is much support for the indigenous system and there is wide acceptance of the modifications which have been introduced by the British. Clash of values is unavoidable in such a situation but the British have been skillful in avoiding violent clashes. Much subtle change has been introduced, and even the opposition now expresses itself in the legal and democratic forms of English Law and Government. I am here interested primarily in the indigenous system, however, and my analysis will be directed to this rather than to analysis of the problems of transition which I view as dependent upon an understanding of what is being transformed.

Chapter III

KINSHIP AND LINEAGE

THE smallest residential grouping recognized by the Shambala is the nuclear family consisting of father, mother, and children. The ideal familial pattern in Shambala terms is the compound polygynous family. Wives and children are regarded as a man's greatest assets and nearly all men strive to fulfil this ideal pattern. Residence is predominantly virilocal; residence with the lineage of a wife is not unknown but is far less common. The difficulty of acquiring land in a wife's village is one major obstacle to such residence, but more importantly virilocal residence is the preferred type of which the Shambala say, 'A boy is like a seed, you can't divide it, but a girl is like a sunflower which is sent out over the country.'

Within this pattern, each nuclear family has a considerable degree of autonomy. Each new wife is properly brought to her husband's village and installed in a house of her own. There are many departures from this pattern, however. Frequently new wives are simply given a separate hearth and storage place within the house of another wife, yet, even when this is done, the distinction between the two units is stringently maintained.

Each of a man's wives should possess separate dwelling space, separate fields, and a clearly demarcated portion of the total stock. Inheritance is of the type known as the 'house-property complex' in which each child inherits from its own mother's portion of the wealth.[1]

The girls receive only a few household utensils, ornaments, and articles of clothing from their mother or sisters who predecease them, while the boys will receive the land and stock allocated to their mother by their father. Such allocation takes place soon after marriage when the new husband shows his wife

---

[1] Max Gluckman, 'Kinship and Marriage Among the Lozi of Northern Rhodesia and the Zulu of Natal', in A. R. Radcliffe-Brown and Daryll Forde, eds., *African Systems of Kinship and Marriage* (London: Oxford University Press, 1950), p. 195.

the field or fields she will have and the stock which will be hers. This will have been tentatively discussed between the groom and the bride's father before the marriage. A man usually retains a part of the land and stock for himself if he has enough. Except in the case of quite wealthy men, this usually means that a man has alloted nearly all of his property to his first wife. If he wishes to marry a second wife, he must not only accumulate stock but also persuade his first wife to give up a part of her fields. He cannot simply take such fields without her permission, for her brothers would be certain to hear of it and make a strong protest, as will the sons if they are adults. The several nuclear families joined by plural marriage are jealous of their rights and no husband would invite trouble by shifting property rights among them without their consent. At present there is an increasing desire among men to retain more land upon which they may grow cash crops. This leads men to attempt to take back land already apportioned to a wife and causes much trouble between husbands and wives. It may also lower the rate of plural marriage although I have no figures which would indicate such an effect.

Each nuclear family is formed through the recognition of a social relationship which may or may not coincide with a physical tie. If a man has failed to perform the recognized marriage ceremonies, the children will belong to the mother's kin. Evidence of legal marriage is the transfer of bride wealth from a man to the father and other kin of the prospective bride. This action should precede the bearing of children but it is not sufficient to establish their legitimacy. It provides the rights of access to the woman, but rights over her children must be further established by subsequent transferals of wealth attendant upon successful live birth. This is begun with the handing over of a female goat to the wife's father when the wife becomes pregnant; a second goat must be sent after the birth of the child. After the birth of a second child, a cow must be sent; this terminates the obligation for subsequent children, except for the goat which precedes each birth, and certain small gifts.

These payments establish the legitimacy of a man's control over his own nuclear family and define the familial membership of his offspring, placing them within a wide kinship grouping in which rights and obligations are clearly defined. This stress

33

upon agnatic relatedness and virilocal residence produces a localized exogamous grouping or lineage which traces descent back to some known founder and is named after this founder. Such patrilineages are given clear recognition by the Shambala as permanently constituted groups and are referred to as the 'house' of this founder, as *Chengo cha Mbira* (house of Mbira). They are very numerous as the result of a continuing process of segmentation. Lineages are linked by real or imputed genealogical ties into a number of patriclans widely dispersed throughout Shambalai.

The smallest such lineage I should like to term the minimum effective lineage. It may be defined in purely empirical terms as the smallest group which is recognized within the society as possessing a name and a territory.[1] The minimum effective lineage appears from the outside as a unit with a recognized leader who deals with other such leaders in the field of external political relations. Within the lineage, authority is largely of a familial nature based upon principles of kinship and age.

The minimum effective lineage usually spans three or four living generations from senior adults of the present and has a total depth of approximately seven to nine generations. An empirical consideration of numbers of Shambala lineages reveals that some achieve a high degree of localization and solidarity while others are scattered. However, the localized corporate lineage appears to be the normative type towards which all lineages approximate. Older informants look back to the days before the Europeans, when they feel everything was in its proper place, and explain that all villages were localized lineages then. This is especially the case when they are confronted with explaining the maze of relationships existing in their own village. Nevertheless it is regarded as the nature of things that lineages will split occasionally when they become very large and that new villages will be formed which may eventually

---

[1] The Shambala minimum effective lineage is considerably different from Fortes' effective minimal lineage, Meyer Fortes, *The Dynamics of Clanship Among the Tallensi* (London: Oxford University Press, 1945), p. 192, even though my term is rather similar. No alternative term could be devised which conveyed the sense of the unit satisfactorily. The effective minimal lineage as delineated among the Tallensi is usually a domestic family whereas in Shambala terms a domestic family is economically, jurally, and ritually subordinated to a larger agnatic unit which is a corporate group forming a village or a part of a village.

become quite separate and possess political autonomy like that of the parent village. Segmentation is proper; dispersion and dissolution is not.

Those lineages which approach this normative type, which act as corporate groups, possess political status. They are entities within the context of a chiefdom which have relations with each other and which comprise the constituents of a chief. However, at any given point in time not all lineages are of this form. In the normal course of events, some lineages proliferate and grow, others break down, and some are in the process of splitting away.

Some lineages are isolated. There exist lineages which trace no agnatic ties wider than among the residents of a single village. Such isolated lineages make up only a small part of all lineages. A far greater proportion of lineages recognize agnatic ties with other lineages and thus form wide groupings called *kolwa* (pl. *makolwa*). Many of these take the form of loose aggregates of parallel lineages which are able to trace genealogical connection only inexactly but which nevertheless claim some common ancestor and may be termed clans.[1]

Rules of exogamy extend to the width of the total clan, though effective action is nearly always limited to the localized lineage. The unity of the group through the claim of common agnatic descent is explicitly recognized by the members of all of its constituent lineages, however, and it possesses a name and a body of oral traditions concerning the life and migrations of its founder and other important ancestors. The genealogical connection to these founders is generally traced in all lineages but is often conflicting between lineages and may be extremely vague and even contradictory in its details. Most of these clans composed of shallow parallel lineages possess no machinery for action on a clan-wide basis. There is no clan head, or council, or the recognition of a senior lineage, or joint ceremonial activity, or clan ownership of property. Clans cannot in any sense be considered corporate groups but are composed of a series of corporate lineages which are the widest units mobilized

---

[1] The clan is defined in *Notes and Queries on Anthropology* (6th rev. edn., London: Routledge and Kegan Paul, 1951), p. 89, as ' . . . a group of persons of both sexes, membership of which is determined by unilineal descent actual or putative with *ipso facto* obligations of an exclusive kind.'

for common action.[1] The lineages which make up such a clan do not usually occupy a stretch of contiguous territory but instead are widely scattered throughout the whole of the mountains and the nearby plains. The members of the various lineages extend hospitality to each other but they do not act together for any joint ends. In a few cases of lineages residing near each other, kin terms may be applied but in general such terms are restricted to members of the individual's localized lineage.

Segmentation and Clan Structure

The reference genealogy diagrammed in figure four was constructed from investigations in different villages occupied by lineages of the same clan. In this case all of the detailed genealogies trace back to an ancestor named Semkale but relationship to Semkale is not clear; in fact, even which Semkale is meant is not clear. I here show it in a form constructed by myself to rid it of major inconsistencies and in terms of a kind of consensus eventually achieved among elders of the various localized lineages. It is possible to get versions from different men in the same lineage or even from the same man on different days which derive from different points in the total genealogy. This has no functional significance to the clan membership however. The important thing for them is that the lineages are agnatically linked. The exact manner is not of importance; the mere fact of linkage is sufficient for reckoning exogamy. Other matters are handled within the constituent lineages. Thus rites of ancestor worship are occasionally directed to the clan founder by each lineage, but more importantly they are directed to the immediate founder of each localized lineage by the living members of the local group. Further, leadership is localized and pertains

[1] Radcliffe-Brown defines a corporate group in *African Systems of Kinship and Marriage* (London: Oxford University Press, 1950), p. 41, as being one which possesses any of the following characteristics. 'If its members, or its adult members, or a considerable proportion of them, come together occasionally to carry out some collective action, for example, the performance of rites; if it has a chief or council who are regarded as acting as the representatives of the group as a whole; if it possesses or controls property which is collective, as when a clan or lineage is a landholding group.' I find this set of criteria so broad as to be of minimum utility, yet this type of Shambala clan is excluded even with such a wide definition, although its constituent lineages clearly are not.

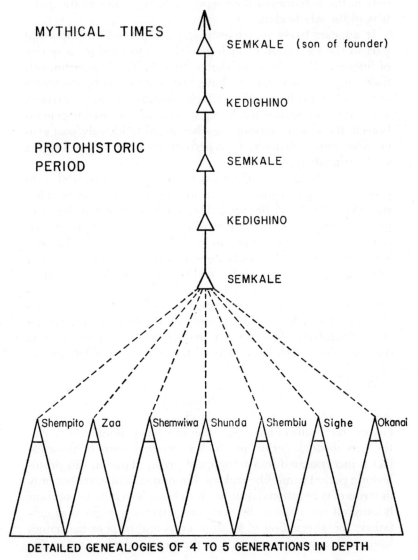

MYTHICAL TIMES

SEMKALE (son of founder)

KEDIGHINO

PROTOHISTORIC
PERIOD

SEMKALE

KEDIGHINO

SEMKALE

Shempito   Zaa   Shemwiwa   Shunda   Shembiu   Sighe   Okanai

DETAILED GENEALOGIES OF 4 TO 5 GENERATIONS IN DEPTH

SCHEMATIC   DIAGRAM OF COMMONER CLAN STRUCTURE

only to the activities of the corporate lineage, not to the members of the whole clan.

It appears likely that telescoping has played an important part in the formation of such genealogies to produce a system of lineages all at the same shallow depth. Tendencies towards fission within these lineages have been countered by the merging of collateral lines which is facilitated by leviratic marriage, while at the same time the strong stress upon alternating generations in the kinship terminology has acted to identify past generations with each other. Thus perhaps the alternation of names in the genealogy.

These factors, plus others discussed below, act together to produce a clan composed of imprecisely but nevertheless strongly articulated lineages. The whole clan has a depth of about seven to nine generations which remains constant because of the continued operation of telescoping. Thus the total genealogy moves forward through time in a manner similar to that discussed for the Nuer by Evans-Pritchard.[1] Unlike Nuer lineages, Shambala clans of the type under discussion are not composed of a hierarchy of segmentary levels in which the oppositions of a lower level create a unity on the level above. Within these Shambala clans there is recognized only one order of segmentation which has produced the series of parallel lineages of which the clans are composed.

Within such clans, the earliest part of the genealogy becomes a sort of formula recalled by all members of all lineages which acts as a charter for the whole clan. These early names lie beyond the limits of historical time in what I should like to call the 'protohistoric period' in which a certain amount of historical fact is incorporated in a complex of myth. Time in this protohistoric period cannot be reckoned in numbers of years but only in terms of generational distance which tends to remain constant because of telescoping. Beyond the generation of great grandfather, the alternation of kinship terms and of personal names leads to a repetition which has the potential of going on in-

---

[1] E. E. Evans-Pritchard, *The Nuer* (London: Oxford University Press, 1940). See especially chap. III, pp. 104–8, and chap. V, pp. 199–200. Here the notion of structural time is clearly laid out and the consequences of its operation in a segmentary society are examined. This idea has been further discussed by Fortes for the Tallensi, Meyer Fortes, *The Dynamics of Clanship among the Tallensi* (London: Oxford University Press, 1945).

definitely but which does not because it is used to express the relation among modern lineage units. This is accomplished through the remembrance of important events of the past and their location in the genealogy, that is, three generations after settlement in the Usambara Mountains, for example. This time is not as precise as the structural time discussed by Evans-Pritchard in his treatment of the Nuer since the complexity and precision of segmentation is not as great as in Nuer lineages. However, the location of events in time is accomplished in so far as this is important to the Shambala.

Beyond these names lies the migration story of the clan in a mythical time which remains in the same perspective because of the genealogies which follow from it. This time is of a different quality than that which follows in lacking any subdivisions. It is vaguely defined, and events sometimes take on a semi-supernatural character. The departure from the homeland is nearly always the result of a quarrel among brothers over cattle or inheritance. The migration is usually fraught with difficulties and sometimes seems to take several generations, but this is not specific and informants cannot agree on the length of time involved. Unanimity and precision with respect to lapsed generations begins with arrival and settlement in the Usambara Mountains. Genealogical dating starts, as it were, with a settlement in Shambalai.

Thus these early histories generally state the reasons for leaving the original homeland, recount a migration, tell of arrival in the Usambaras and perhaps give some details of dispersal in the mountains. They almost always explain settlement in the present locale and give details of how land was acquired. In this respect they offer justification for the present distribution of land and for the control exercised over it by the incumbent lineage. The whole constitutes what Malinowski has called a 'pragmatic charter' of the existing situation.[1] Such traditions are widely known and can be quoted by members of nearby lineages of other clans and by chiefs. They are clearly recognized as clarifying rights over land and defining the *status quo*.

Isolated lineages and clans composed of aggregates of parallel lineages do not exhaust the range of variation within the

---

[1] B. Malinowski, 'Myth in Primitive Psychology', in *Magic, Science and Religion, and Other Essays* (Boston: Beacon Press, 1948), p. 79.

Shambala system, although they are very numerous. I have no accurate knowledge of the total number of Shambala clans and lineages for I was unable to accomplish a total census of the Shambala, but I counted more than forty clans most of which contained at least three localized lineages in the regions where I carried out intensive investigations and I was told by informants in those areas that there were other clans which were not represented by lineages in the areas where I worked. Although the vast majority of clans are of the type made up of parallel lineages, at least two are of a more highly organized segmentary nature. Clans of this last type form systems of several orders of segmentation in which the relations between lineages at one level are defined in terms of solidarity at a higher level of segmentation. The royal clan, schematically represented in figure five, is the outstanding example of such a system. In addition, there is at least one commoner clan which displays this type of organization and which significantly plays an important role in the organization of the total society.

As is true in most social systems, the groups which emerge vary according to the activity at hand. The emphasis upon the span of the lineage which is mobilized depends upon the activities in which individuals are engaged at any one time. Within a segmentary system units emerge in their opposition to other units of a similar nature. Thus it is possible as Fortes has done, to distinguish what he has called minimal lineages composed of the children of one father as distinct from the children of another father.[1] Such minimal lineages have a reality in those actions in which they engage as unique groups but they also go to make up a larger group of no less reality in their participation together in activities at a higher level of segmentation. Activities at this level are the result of participation by representatives of all of the constituent parts of the entity as defined by the genealogies which articulate these parts. The units which emerge depend directly upon the occasion and the genealogical definition of who shall be involved.

Within the Shambala system, the minimal lineage of Fortes does not generally emerge as a group although it has the potentiality of emerging through opposition to other similar

---

[1] Meyer Fortes, *The Dynamics of Clanship among the Tallensi* (London: Oxford University Press, 1945), pp. 30–1.

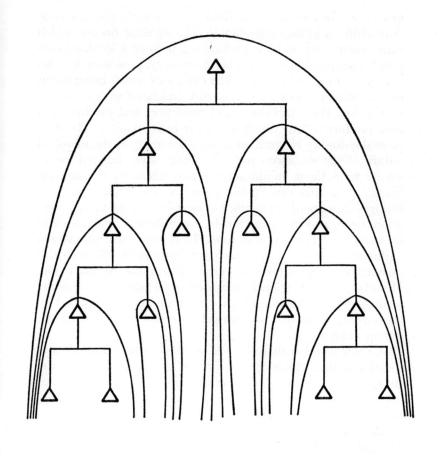

 SEGMENT BOUNDARY

SCHEMATIC DIAGRAM OF LINEAGE SEGMENTS IN
THE ROYAL CLAN.

groups, as, for instance, in a dispute over inheritance or succession within a village community. The smallest lineage which consistently emerges is that which has become a localized corporate group holding a recognized territory, possessing a clear-cut leadership, and a name. The situations which bring about its recognition are of a constant sort associated with economic production, the establishment of residence, and the like, and they produce a unit which has a persistent reality. The constant day-to-day recognition of such groups and the manifold nature of the situations which mobilize them has led me to earlier term them 'minimum effective lineages', the smallest lineage groupings usually recognized by the Shambala. Such lineages vary greatly in depth, but most are at least three generations deep, and many are far deeper, although new units will be established from time to time. Thus most have submerged within them a number of lineages of lesser span which receive no effective recognition in the normal day-to-day routine of life. However, it is along such lines that segmentation may occur leading to the formation of new corporate lineages founded by an out-migration of a submerged potential lineage from the parent village.

In contexts other than those of the day-to-day economic and social activities which occupy most of the people most of the time, lineages of greater span crystallize. Many such occasions are ceremonial in nature and have to do with ancestor worship, mourning, or rites of passage. Here under the aegis of certain kinds of circumstances different and broader alignments are brought into play. The referents for such alignments are the points of convergent ascent deemed significant in terms of the genealogies of the various minimum effective lineages, that is, the points of segmentation which have produced these various lineages. A segment at any level has its focus of unity in the ancestor by reference to whom it is differentiated from other segments at the same level. Observances directed to this ancestor call for the presence of representatives of all the segments below which trace to this ancestor. Thus the context determines the unit of action.

The unity achieved in clans of this third type is of a much higher order than that displayed in the majority of Shambala clans. In most clans there is no means of mobilizing the dis-

4. Mixed fields of maize, beans, cassava and plantains surround most villages. Note that the village is located on the highest point of the ridge. The nearest water is approximately half a mile away.

5. Land is often heavily scarred by erosion in the immediate vicinity of a village because of the daily movement of stock to pasturage. Euphorbia trees have been planted as hedges around this village.

6. The modern style of rectangular houses predominates in this portion of the *kitala* of Mlalo. Note the plantain gardens interplanted among the rather closely spaced houses.

7. A traditional round house with untrimmed thatch which is allowed to extend to the ground. This house is a *nyumba nkuu* or house of chiefly relics.

persed minimum effective lineages for any kind of joint action. The vague feeling of unity and the possession of a common name are the major things shared. On the other hand, the possession of genealogies which exactly define the relations between parts of a clan and the possession of an ideology which calls for joint action from time to time on the basis of these relations, produces a structure of widely ramifying dimensions in clans of the third type.

The size of the segment mobilized varies greatly depending on the circumstances, but it acts as a unit when so mobilized. The Shambala recognize the existence of segments of varying span and inclusiveness but they do not distinguish among them terminologically. In the Shambala view there are only two kinds of units: the total clan which they term *kolwa* (pl. *makolwa*) and a segment of a total clan or *chengo* (pl. *vyengo*).

A lineage of any span less than the clan as a whole is a *chengo*. It is at first confusing to the fieldworker to be told that the membership of a village is a *chengo* and then to find a few days later that representatives of a dozen villages gathered together for a mourning is a *chengo*, and still later to witness rites of ancestor worship at which members of twenty villages are present and find that this is also a *chengo*. Genealogical materials soon make it clear, however, that these simply represent progressively higher orders of segmentation and that the application of the same term to all is in fact an accurate reflection of the relative nature of lineage affiliation.

Ancestor Worship

The rituals of ancestor worship are one of the contexts within which Shambala ideas of lineage unity and segmentation emerge. Ceremonies directed to the ancestors are differentiated from other classes of ceremonies by the Shambala and are termed *mufika* or *muviga*. *Mufika* are of considerable importance, for the dead are not gone but rather are still somehow present and ready to take an active interest in the affairs of the living. They are often indifferent, sometimes benevolent, but likely to be troublesome if ignored too long. In any case they are capricious in their actions. Every man should provide his deceased father with a proper sacrifice approximately once in every full agricultural cycle and at any other time a diviner advises. Any kind of misfortune—sickness, crop failure, stock loss, serious arguments in the village—is likely to be the wage of ignoring the ancestors.

In the event of any such misfortune a diviner will probably be consulted to find out what is responsible for the trouble. Diviners generally answer initial questions concerning the cause of trouble and determine the form that corrective rituals should take. The source of trouble is usually some powerful male ancestor such as one's father or grandfather, but it may be some more remote ancestor and it is possible that it could be even the spirit of a child or a woman. It is not infrequently suggested that a person in trouble should have his mother's brother appeal to his ancestors. Ancestors in the mother's line may bring one trouble quite as easily as those in father's line but do so less frequently.

No man may sacrifice directly to his more remote ancestors as long as his father or other men of the minimum effective lineage who are senior to him are alive. Women can never sacrifice to the ancestors and should not even be present when offerings are made. The lineage head should sacrifice on behalf of the lineage members regularly and should also conduct any rites advised for some junior member of the lineage by a diviner. The individual for whom the ceremony is done must provide a small gift for the intermediary. However, any man may sacrifice to his own deceased father privately and without the presence of anyone but his own sons. Such an observance is now fairly rare and is done only in cases of grave misfortune. Few men regularly invoke the aid and protection of their ancestors, but only do so in response to difficulties. Nevertheless, ancestor worship is one of the most important tasks in which lineage affiliation is reinforced.

Within the majority of Shambala clans, each minimal effective lineage conducts its ancestor ceremonies separately. Such observances are done within the village, but at no sort of shrine, and are directed to the founder of the particular lineage, although the clan founder is mentioned as well. A regular verbal formula is employed which begins with the clan founder, mentions the founder of the lineage, and may mention other more immediate ancestors if the diviner has pinpointed any.

44

The observances are essentially the same for those clans of a more elaborate segmentary nature but depart in several respects. In clans of this type, it is expected that the rite will involve all those segments which are reckoned as descending from the ancestor to be invoked. It appears that it is not necessary for every man to attend, but a representative from every segment should attend. In most cases this means that lineage heads will gather and that the ceremony will then be conducted by the head of the senior lineage present. Under these circumstances the gathering represents a lineage of a higher order of segmentation composed of numbers of lesser segments reckoned as a separate for other tasks. Such a ceremony should take place in the village of the senior segment, which is usually the site of the burial of the ancestor in question.

Occasionally such ceremonies are directed to the founder of the whole clan and to him alone. The traditions of the clan include specification of the site first settled by this founder which is regarded as a sacred place and is referred to as *tongo*. If the rite is to the clan founder, it is at the *tongo* that it must be conducted and it is proper that the heads of all the constituent lineages should attend.

A ceremony such as this should be conducted by the senior lineal descendent of the clan founder. I never observed an ancestor ceremony of these dimensions, and I could not find many men who had. One of my best informants on such matters, an old man and head of a large lineage, could only claim to have visited the *tongo* of his clan twice for such rites. He explained that in most cases there was no longer any village at the *tongo* site, the place having been abandoned for some reason. Further questioning on this point made it appear that loss of soil fertility through long use was the probable reason for such abandonment. Nevertheless, the site is specified in oral tradition and marked by a sacred grove or tree. When clan elders assemble there they construct a temporary house of poles and brush in circular form to shelter the ceremony. This house must be erected in one day and roofed by nightfall. The ceremonies to the clan founder are carried out that night and the following day. On the third day the house is burnt down and black goats and bulls which have been sacrificed by strangulation are eaten. On the fourth day all of the participants return home. The royal clan as well as some commoner clans practice this type of ceremony. The royal *tongo* is the village of Shashui, still occupied by commoner lineages, which served as the residence away from the capital for Mbega and contains the graves of Mbega, Buge, Shebuge and Kimweri Mkubwa as well as other royal chiefs of lower rank. Thus curiously, Vuga, although the *Kitala Kikuu* or capital, does not contain the graves of its chiefs which lie three miles away. Many young men had never witnessed such large ceremonies as those held at a *tongo*. Of course, this is partially due to the fact that relatively few Shambala clans are organized in a manner which calls for such ceremonies, but even within those that possess this type of organization the ceremonies are rare.

Rites of ancestor worship are of extreme importance within the royal clan and are practiced with more frequency than appears to be the case in commoner clans. A part of every royal village is a special fenced inclosure within which are buried the royal chiefs of that village. Such an inclosure, called a *kigiri*, is the scene of much royal ancestor ritual. Associated with the *kigiri* is the official residence of the chief, called the *nyumba ya mufika* (house of ancestor observances) or simply *nyumba nkuu* (big house). Within this house are kept relics of past chiefs. These include a large drum associated with the soul of the ruling chief, stools, spears, swords, shields, and ritual paraphernalia of previous chiefs. Both the house and the burial inclosure are sacred to the ancestor cult of the royal lineage centered in the particular village, and a considerable body of ritual and of ritual prohibition (*miko*) surrounds them. This complex of royal burial plot and sacred house is termed *kitala*. In common usage, the term *kitala* is used to refer to the royal village in general, but in proper usage can only mean a village in which the relics of royal chiefs are kept. A new royal village is not actually a *kitala* until it contains such relics and has become sacred within the royal ancestor cult. Before the death and burial of the founder of a new royal village the royal clansmen of that village could not conduct ancestor ceremonies but would go to the village of their origin for ceremonies. I would suggest that the segmentation is not viewed as complete until the death of this man.

The presence of such concrete manifestations of the ancestor cult gives a clarity to the segmentations of the royal clan which is lacking to some extent in commoner clans. Attention to the ancestors is more of a day-to-day occurrence when there is a burial place in the middle of the village and when one must observe certain ritual prohibitions constantly. Failure to observe these prohibitions requires the sacrifice of a sheep and an explanation to the ancestors; entrance into the *nyumba nkuu* calls for utterance of a verbal formula and other prescribed actions. These serve as ever present reminders of the ancestors, and this in turn reinforces the genealogical framework of the royal clan. The segmentations of the royal clan as marked by the ancestors thus honored are common knowledge. Any informant, regardless of his clan, can trace many of the most important segmentations in the royal clan, although knowledge of the details of royal genealogies is restricted to members of the royal lineage in question and to a few elders of other lineages intimately associated with it.

The form of ancestor worship within the royal clan is closely intertwined with political organization. Indeed the two can only be analytically separated, for shrines are only erected for those royal ancestors who attain political importance. This they do by either succeeding to an established chiefship or by establishing a new chiefship in an area where none previously existed. Thus it appears that only royal lineages possessing ancestor shrines may be viewed as corporate groups. The shrine is an index of the corporateness of the unit. This does not mean that royal ancestors who did not become chiefs are not important; rather, that they are simply conceived as being usually included in any worship which occurs at the shrine to those who did become chiefs. Such ancestors may be explicitly mentioned by name in an ancestor ritual if a diviner has so suggested. The individuals who assemble for such a ritual, however, are for most tasks submerged within some larger corporate entity which has achieved political recognition through a chiefship, a name, and identification with a range of territory.

Figure six is a reference genealogy of the royal chiefs within the modern subchiefdom of Mlado. The major chiefs of the area descend in a direct line from the founder of the chiefship in this region of the mountains. The incumbent chief, Hassani, still resides at the burial site of the lineage founder, Daffa, and is in

47

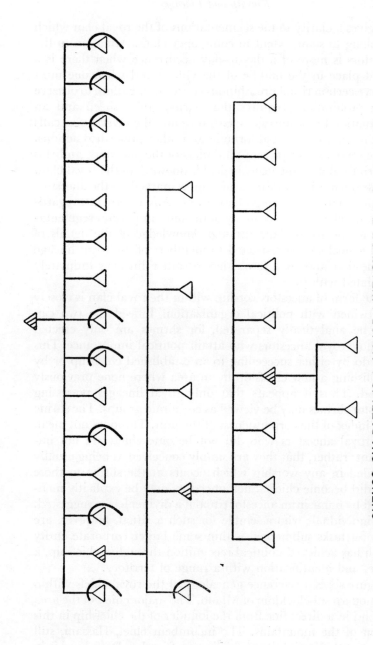

CHENGO CHA DAFFA IS A MAJOR LINEAGE OF THE ROYAL CLAN.
SEGMENTATIONS SHOWN THUS ⟩   MAJOR CHIEFS ◬

SCHEMATIC DIAGRAM OF THE ROYAL LINEAGE OF MLALO

48

charge of the ancestor shrine. The only other royal ancestor shrines within the subchiefdom are those maintained by the minimum effective lineages within the major segment, that is, by the various segments which have splintered off through the establishment of lesser chieftaincies within the subchiefdom.

The Corporate Lineage

Not only does lineage unity emerge in the religious context of ancestor worship, but the persistent reality of the minimum effective lineage is seen in many other contexts. The localized lineage possesses rights in property which appear to be based on the principles that: (1) prior occupation, that is, first opening of new land and settlement on it, is evidence of exclusive rights to land except where abrogated by the burial of a royal chief whose spirit then animates the land, (2) such rights are inherited patrilineally by the male descendants of the first settler.

The opening of land upon which no prior claim exists confers full rights and such land may be alienated by the pioneer. However, at his death such rights in land pass to the lineage he has founded by his migration. The corporate right of this lineage is confirmed during the formal mourning for the deceased by a meeting and division of the land. Any land or other wealth conferred on others by the deceased prior to his death is simply affirmed at this time, other lands he held are apportioned by wives' households in usufruct tenure to his sons and failing sons, to his brothers or grandsons. Land inherited within the lineage cannot be alienated since there is a lineage right in it. Grazing land and houseplots also cannot be alienated, the former always being held jointly and the latter, although held by the resident during his occupation, always reverting to the lineage at vacation to be disposed of in joint council. The house materials themselves, however, are privately owned by the builder.

These principles are well demonstrated in cases heard before the Native Court of *Zumbe Mkuu* Hassani of Mlalo in 1957.

Rashidi and Asmani claimed a field being worked by Billa. They brought as witnesses three brothers of their father who testified that their deceased brother had worked the land and that it had been divided between Rashidi and Asmani at the death of their

49

father. Billa brought two councillors to the chief as witnesses who had witnessed the father's sale of the land to Billa and who further testified that the land was first brought under cultivation by the father and had not been inherited by him. The court affirmed the father's right to sell it and awarded the holding to Billa.

On the other hand, lineage rights to land were affirmed in the following case.

Hassani claimed a field which was being worked by Adamu. He produced two witnesses who had been present when he bought it from the deceased father of Adamu. Adamu claimed that his father had, in fact, no right to sell it since he had inherited it from Adamu's grandfather (the deceased's father) and brought as witnesses two elders of his lineage who had been present at the mourning ceremonies for the grandfather when land was re-apportioned. The court held that Hassani's purchase was not binding and awarded the field to Adamu.

Not only do lineage members possess joint rights in property but they are also morally and jurally responsible for each other's action. The following case illustrates the position of the lineage rather closely:

When I was a small boy my father's brother was cutting a tree in the bush one day when he saw a kind of vine that grows wild there. He stopped cutting and went to dig its roots, which are very good. While he was gone, a girl passed by on the path and the tree which he had been cutting fell on her. He came home and said nothing, but they found the girl and some others who had seen him go to cut wood said that he had killed her.

The chief was angry because the girl was of his lineage, but he did not kill my father's brother but sent him to the paramount chief. The paramount chief ordered him to pay murder compensation (*kimba*, a fine of twelve cattle). My father's brother did not have so many cattle so the paramount chief said, 'Your *chengo* must pay the *kimba*.' My father's brother quickly gave my two sisters to men who had spoken to him of them and my father and the others paid the rest of the cattle because we would be ashamed and our cattle taken anyway if we had not.

The men of my *chengo* were angry about paying for the mistake of my father's brother and everyone watched him to see that he did not cause more trouble, for it was not the first time that he had done a foolish thing. It was said that he should be told to leave before we would pay again for him, but he never made any more trouble. I had to wait a long time before I married, though, because we had no cattle.

This case brings the legal status of the lineage clearly into focus. Coercion has been brought to bear by the chief upon one kin group for an offense upon another kin group. This force has been brought to bear by persons clearly recognized to possess the authority to make such judgments. It has been exercised, however, beyond the kin but within the political group; the sanctions for such law are not a matter of kinship but are expressly political in nature. One kin group has received compensation *as a group* from another group, *as a group*. Which lineage member had inflicted the injury was not so important as the fact that some lineage member had done so. It was important to the lineage itself, however, and here familial authority was mobilized. That is, the members of the lineage considered expelling the offender, although in this case they did not carry it out.

The lineage is a legal entity within a field of lineages. Here the actions of the lineage member are taken to represent the lineage as a body and here the chief acts to regulate relations between units. The rectification of wrongs is lineage business, and the responsibility for wrongs is a lineage responsibility.

The lineage members are concerned with the moral behavior of their lineage mates, however. Within the lineage the delineation of proper modes of behavior and the enforcement of such behavior is a matter of kinship position and generational seniority. Although the lineage acts as a unit with respect to non-members it is highly differentiated internally. This may be partly understood through a consideration of the kinship terminology and the behavior which accompanies its application. A wide range of usage provides a coherent and relatively permanent classificatory structure. Terms applied are extended to a broad range of kin, although the nuances of behavior are less closely defined as the genealogical distance increases.

Emphasis is placed upon the paternal kin with whom one lives and works. Nevertheless, the individual recognizes links with the families of both parents. The terminology reflects this through the wide application of terms for cognatic kin which are identical with those applied to agnatic kin. The most important

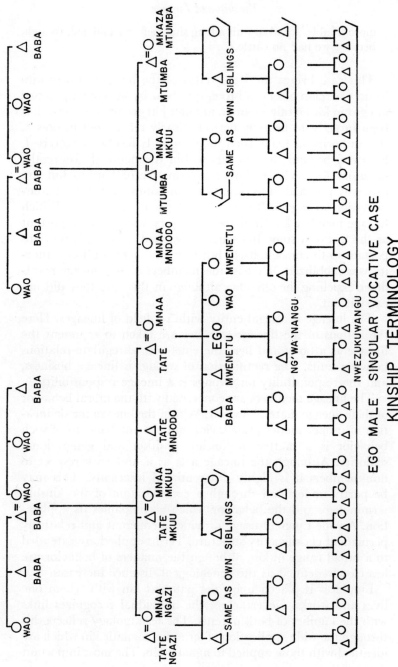

KINSHIP TERMINOLOGY

EGO MALE SINGULAR VOCATIVE CASE

kin relations outside of one's agnatic group are with matri-lateral cross cousins and with mother's brother. Mother's brother, as a senior representative of mother's lineage, represents the maternal ancestors and also has obligations to help with the bride wealth for sister's son. This is stressed by terminologically setting him off from other maternal kin. Matrilateral cross cousins, on the other hand, are called by the same terms as own siblings and are treated in similar fashion to siblings.

The general form of the extended kinship structure may be seen on the accompanying chart.[1] Of utmost importance in the terminology are distinctions based upon generation and relative age within generations. Thus all siblings and cousins are distin-guished as to whether they are older or younger than self. This is of great importance to inheritance and the right to claim bride wealth. It is considered proper that a man's eldest son should succeed to any political office which the man may hold, and although this is not a hard and fast rule, elder sons far more frequently inherit offices than do younger sons. Furthermore, elder sons have first claim on property allocated to their mother for payment of bride wealth. Junior sons may not marry until their more senior full brothers have done so or have specific-ally waived their first rights (as they sometimes do in this age of labor migration). This affects the distribution of property among sons since each son is given cattle and other wealth upon marriage. At the death of the father the remainder of his wealth is divided equally within each group of full brothers, irrespective of the allocations which were made at the marriage of each son. Thus junior sons not yet married will have to share equally with senior sons who already possess a prior share gained at marriage.

[1] The system is of the type Murdock has called Guinea because of its prevalence in West Africa. G. P. Murdock, *Social Structure* (New York: MacMillan, 1949), pp. 224-5, 235-6. This type of system is distinguished by the recognition of exogamous patrilineal lineages with a cousin terminology of either the Eskimo or Hawaiian types. The Shambala case is characterized by Hawaiian cousin terminology. That is, all cross and parallel female cousins are called by the same terms as those used for sisters. Murdock views the Guinea system as a transition from either the bilateral Eskimo or Hawaiian types where patrilocal residence has led to the development of patrilineal descent. There is no evidence other than the existence of the system itself that this has been the course of events in Shambalai. The lack of detailed historical records of any depth precludes any attempt to test Murdock's hypothesis in this case.

Not only is age within a generation stressed in the terminology, it is also important between generations. The terminology stresses the alternation of generations, classing males of ego's generation with males of grandfather's, and females of ego's generation with grandmother's. Males and females of the first ascending generation are classed with males and females of the third ascending generation, and, finally, members of the first and third descending generation are classed together as are members of the second and fourth descending generation.

Formality and distance is maintained between adjacent generations but alternate generations are on terms of familiarity and companionship. If a young man is having difficulty in getting his father to arrange his marriage, he may appeal to his grandfather for aid. The grandfather and other members of his generation are usually able to exert enough pressure to force the father into providing the necessary stock, but if they cannot the grandfather may assume the obligation himself and collect later from his son. This kind of help and support occurs frequently even when boys are small.[1]

The ties between father and son are close and strong, but etiquette demands formality and respect. A man may not eat with his father, sit while his father stands, call him loudly by name, make bawdy jokes in his presence, or disobey his orders. Failure to observe this pattern can lead to an open breach, or disinheritance, or—most seriously—to a father's curse. Extreme disobedience and the flouting of parental authority is taken very seriously, and a father's curse is a strong sanction, far stronger than disinheritance. It is not lightly invoked or easily retracted, and it tempers relations even when the chance of its invocation is remote and unlikely. Fathers apparently have considerable ambivalence in their feeling towards their sons. The fear that a son will disobey and put them in the position of uttering a curse seems to be a major factor in maintaining distance between a man and his sons. Sons, on the other hand, need cattle and land from their fathers and press hard against the reluctance of father to give up his wealth for their advantage.

This dilemma is becoming increasingly painful as cash

---

[1] Such relations are very common; see the discussion by Radcliffe-Brown in A. R. Radcliffe-Brown and D. Forde, eds., *African Systems of Kinship and Marriage* (London: Oxford University Press, 1950), pp. 27–9.

cropping becomes more important and widespread. It is particularly the case with land that has been planted in such crops as coffee which effect a long-term improvement and which involve considerable investments in cash and labor. The cash proceeds from the sale of a crop like coffee represent the means of entrance to a new series of statuses and the acquisition of new symbols of status for a man, while at the same time, there is still involvement in a traditional status system in which the provision of ample wealth for a son's marriage is a highly valued act. This, of course, also meant in the past that sons would have the means, and feel the obligation, of caring for elderly fathers. Here was the crux of the ancient dilemma, the passing of land and cattle to sons could mean the passing out of an active role for a man as he then became dependent on his sons. This is made more painful at the present by the weakening of the older order in which the high status of age might offset the sting of economic dependence.

The formality and distance between adjacent generations is much stronger between males than between boys and their mothers, men and their daughters, or daughter and mother. This formality approximates a kind of semi-avoidance at about the age of puberty when boys must leave home to live in the bachelor's house which is part of every village. From this time until marriage they are in their father's and mother's house only to visit, get food, or when sick or injured. Even when small, children are taught to ask before entering the hut and only to visit the inner room where mother and father sleep at the invitation of their parents. Even so, young children are fondled and played with by their father and are rarely disciplined by him unless their transgressions are of an extremely grave nature. The shift of father's role at puberty is an extremely far-reaching event in a boy's life, and it signalizes a situation which prevails until father's death in which he represents the authority of seniority with its control over land, the right to marry, and political power. When a man has reached middle age and has acquired wealth of his own, he still publicly accedes to the wishes of his father's generation, though he may subvert these covertly or grumble to his peers over their foolishness. Not only does he respect the wishes of father's generation, but he also continues to observe certain kinds of avoidances. This emerged clearly to me at a feast which I gave upon leaving one area of the mountains to work elsewhere. I invited many informants, chiefs, and councillors whom I had interviewed and known as friends without thinking that they were from three generational levels. My cook was filled with pride over the prospect and began organizing everything in proper traditional manner. However, he was aghast when he got a full list of the men invited and quickly pointed out that fathers and sons would never eat together. After much discussion it was decided that all would be well if the generations were placed in separate locations and proper attention was payed to precedence in serving the food and in allocating the pieces of meat. The separation was even more rigid for the beer drinking which followed and no generation wished any younger generation to observe them while drinking.

Lineage leadership is determined through the action of these principles of kinship and age. A lineage head is explicitly recognized and is called *mgosh wa chengo* (elder of the house). The position is generally attained through direct inheritance from father to senior son, thus eliminating the claim of collaterals to the position. However, such a leader is chosen by consensus among all the adult male lineage members. Leadership thus can pass to a junior son or to a brother of the deceased or retired leader. It should be held by a mature man and will almost certainly pass to a man of the deceased's generation if there are only young or otherwise unqualified sons to inherit.

These principles are illustrated in the following case of the *chengo cha mbelia* shown in figure eight. Mbelia founded the lineage by migrating to the Usambaras from the Pare Mountains. His first son, Sekeni, followed him as lineage leader but had no male heirs. Thus Sekeni's brother Nyaki became lineage head at Sekeni's death. Nyaki's son Kitojo succeeded to the position which in turn was inherited by his first son, Mkale. Mkale died early while his children were small, and his wife and children were inherited through leviratic marriage by Mkale's brother Nyaki, who became lineage head. Nyaki retired from the position and it passed to his real son, Baro. Baro has left to work and his children are all quite young, so the position has now passed to Sengasu, the son of Mkale but also the son of Nyaki through the operation of the levirate. Genealogies such as this

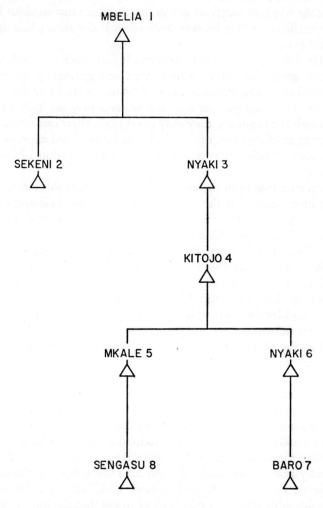

NUMERALS INDICATE ORDER OF SUCCESSION TO LINEAGE LEADERSHIP

LINEAGE LEADERSHIP IN CHENGO CHA MBELIA

example indicate that the criteria of adulthood, good judgment, and the like may override direct descent from the previous head as qualifications for lineage leadership if the direct heir is not suitable.

The lineage head may be regarded as a focus for the solidarity of the group. Nevertheless he cannot be regarded as occupying a position of sole authority. All adult males are involved in the decision making process and the women play an indirect role through the influence they may exert upon their husbands. The lineage leader seldom makes decisions himself, but expresses the currents of opinion which emerge from discussion of lineage affairs.

An example from my own experience makes this clear. During interviews with the *mgosh wa chengo* of the Wanango clan, he informed me that he had a number of very sacred ancestor relics of that clan which were kept in his house by virtue of his position. He described these as a sacred hat, stool, spear, fly switch, and other things. I expressed interest in seeing these relics but he put me off. Three further visits still had not brought the relics into view and I heard from other sources that there was considerable unhappiness with the lineage leader for having offered information about the relics to me.

Finally on a fourth visit, I was met by about fifteen very senior men and a long debate ensued after I explained my desire to view the sacred relics. After much pausing four of the men including the leader arose and informed me that I could view the things which they would bring out but that I would have to offer a small amount of tobacco to the stool as a sacrifice. They then entered the house and remained inside for a long interval which someone suggested was taken up with prayers. They finally reappeared and the men all took turns explaining the objects, their uses, original owners, and antiquity. There was considerable effort to make it clear to me that the lineage leader only 'guarded' the things and that they 'belonged' to all the members of the lineage.

Similarly, as the Shambala express it, the *mgosh wa chengo* 'owns' the lands of the lineage. However, this means that he and his peers in the lineage allocate building sites within the village and unopened agricultural lands around the village. Land alloted by former lineage heads is largely outside of the control of the present head except that he presides at its division among the heirs of a deceased holder and can act to evict an occupant under certain circumstances. If some lineage member is a chronic troublemaker either within the lineage or in the society at large, he may be expelled from the lineage providing all of the adult male members of the lineage agree to such a course. If this is done his lands will be seized and redistributed to other lineage members. Such exiles are sometimes welcomed back in later years, but this is not the understanding when they are forced out. In the past they are usually given to a chief. This meant that the offender and his family became slaves to the chief. The chief then received bride wealth for the daughters and paid bride wealth for the sons and accepted responsibility like that of his own lineage for them. Such formal expulsion of a lineage member is carried out by the lineage head but only after a consensus is apparent within the lineage. The lineage head has no such authority himself.

This is not to say the lineage leader has no authority. His genealogical position confers upon him considerable influence. All younger men and men of generations junior to his own are expected quickly to defer to opinions he may hold simply through the operation of the principles of deference and respect which exist between senior and junior individuals. Furthermore, he is regarded as the intermediary between his lineage and non-lineage members. Thus royal chiefs and heads of other lineages will approach him in any matter which involves his total lineage or any member of it. Legal disputes, marriage arrangements, the conclusion of a pact of blood brotherhood, or nearly any other formal arrangement concluded by a lineage member is attended by the lineage head who is either a witness or a participant.

The control which the *mgosh wa chengo* exercises over ancestor worship greatly strengthens his position. It is the lineage leader who carries out such ceremonies for the lineage members. His refusal to conduct them for some member of the lineage is a distinct possibility if he judges that the individual has not acted in proper and acceptable ways. However, a lineage leader would not take such drastic action without the clear agreement of other members of the lineage. It is not his sole right to refuse ceremonies but rather a major means by which the lineage membership may control a recalcitrant individual. A lineage leader who attempted to withhold the right of ancestor worship on his own initiative would run the risk of being repudiated and replaced by his lineage.

Chapter IV

THE VILLAGE

A Shambala village consists of a collection of wattle and daub huts of various sizes. Many of the huts are rectangular, fifteen to twenty feet long, and ten to fifteen feet wide, with thatched roofs. Others are round and about ten feet in diameter. The rectangular style is said to be modern. Elderly informants claim that it was introduced by the example of German houses. Many of the huts are quite substantially made, and it is claimed that this too is modern. Raiding and warfare dictated small flimsy houses which could be rebuilt easily because they were often burnt down.

Villages vary from collections of perhaps eight to ten huts up to towns of over a hundred huts. Often the huts are only a few yards apart and are located on the brow of a hill, but sometimes they may be widely scattered. Such scattering is easy with the cessation of warfare, since palisades and proximity are no longer needed for protection. In general there is no set pattern to the internal arrangement of a village, although each should contain a bachelor's house for young men. Most villages have fairly clear-cut boundaries, although some interdigitate and cannot be distinguished by an outsider. Villagers themselves see no difficulty here and have a clear conception of the boundaries. They see the village as a social unit, and its spatial boundaries are easily framed from this referent.

The village is first and foremost a lineage unit, but the network of kinship ties is often very diverse. The principle of patrilineal descent is of great importance in organizing the village, and many small villages are made up largely of lineage mates and their spouses. The immediate verbal response to a question about village composition is that the male residents of a village are all members of a lineage. Most large villages, and many smaller ones, depart to some degree from this conceptual pattern. Nevertheless, the genealogical links between village residents form the fabric of village life.

Types of Villages

Three major types of villages may be distinguished. The simplest form is the village occupied by only one commoner lineage. Such villages often contain one or more men of other lineages, but except for the spouses of the adult male lineage members there is no large group of individuals who do not belong to the lineage which holds the land upon which the village is built. By far the most frequent form of commoner village is somewhat more complex in composition. Such villages, which may be called multi-lineage villages, possess a core-patrilineage which is dominant because of its claim of prior occupation of the site. In addition to this dominant lineage, there are one or more other lineages in residence. These lineages often develop from uxorilocal residence in which the sons of the man who has married in are allowed to keep the land that their mother received after her marriage. Such lineages may be said to have secondary rights in land because it is generally well known that they possess land at the sufferance of the dominant lineage which stands in a kind of mother's brother relation to them. There may be several lineages in this relation to the dominant lineage, and it is sometimes the case that one or more of them is numerically larger than the dominant lineage.

This process of uxorilocal residence may occur with respect to a secondary lineage so that still another lineage develops which holds land granted by a secondary lineage. This lineage may be termed a tertiary holder in land rights. Both the secondary and tertiary lineages must defer to the primary occupants in the decision making process in the village. Each lineage will have its own *mgosh wa chengo*, but the leader of the original lineage takes precedence and exercises control over joint activities within the village. Such men are sometimes quite powerful if they lead large villages, and many are now recognized by the Administration on the same footing as the lowest level of royal chiefs although they would have been under these lesser royal chiefs in former times.

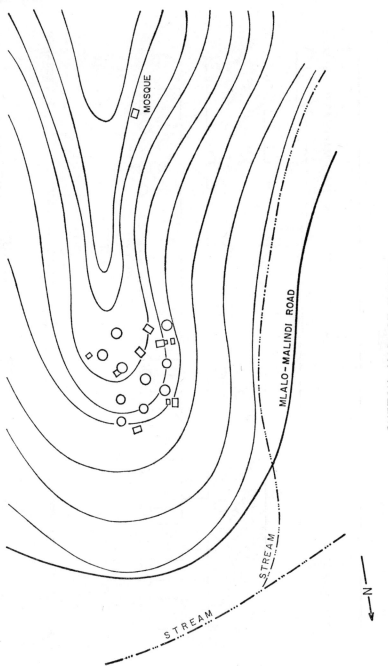

MOSQUE

MLALO-MALINDI ROAD

STREAM

STREAM

N

SKETCH MAP OF YUMBU

DIAGRAM OF KINSHIP IN YUMBU

UNMARRIED CHILDREN ARE NOT NAMED — — — — LEVIRATIC MARRIAGE

△ DECEASED

64

A third type of village is the *kitala*, or royal village. All of the royal villages which I investigated were multi-lineage villages, but unlike the commoner multi-lineage village the royal lineage takes precedence regardless of whether it was the first to settle. Royal villages are always the site of a chiefly residence, a royal burial inclosure, and a house containing ceremonial objects and ancestor relics. These things make them sacred and subject to various kinds of ritual prohibitions (called *miko*) as well as making them the site of public rituals of the royal ancestor cult.

Figure ten is a diagram of the composition of Yumbu, a small village of the simplest type with a total population of 57, composed of members of only one commoner lineage and their spouses. The living membership spans four generations. The village was founded approximately fifty years ago by Mhandavumo, the father of Shehiza, the oldest living member, when Shehiza himself was a young bachelor. Its founding marks a segmentation of an older lineage in a nearby village, with which ties are still important. Nevertheless, it is now recognized as separate and Shehiza is called *mgosh wa chengo*.

Leviratic marriage is important within Shambala kinship and can be seen to be of utmost importance in defining the membership of this village. Three of the adult men now resident in the village, Asmani, Rashidi, and Selemani, are sons of Kupe, a deceased brother of Shehiza, but were inherited by Shehiza through his leviratic marriage with their mother, Kupe's widow. In their version of the lineage genealogy they trace from Shehiza as their father. They have merged a collateral line and produced a fictionalized genealogy consistent with the terms they commonly apply to other individuals within the lineage. Only Shehiza of all members of the village gave a version of his genealogy which placed these men as sons of Kupe. This merging of collateral lines will probably be completely forgotten with Shehiza's death, and the new genealogy which conforms to the relations extant between village residents will be the only one known in the village. When confronted with Shehiza's account all three agreed he probably knew better than they, but a recheck by my clerk several months later elicited the version of the genealogy they had originally given rather than Shehiza's version.

A similar set of circumstances is likely to develop with regard to Hassani the grandson of Shehiza's brother, Selehe. Hassani's version of his genealogy lists Shehiza as his grandfather, while his father Bakari, his grandmother Makiniassi, and Shehiza all gave versions corresponding to that shown in the diagram. Here Hassani has been placed in the relation of grandson to Shehiza not simply by classificatory extension of kin terms but also through leviratic marriage, and has himself assumed that he is the actual grandson of Shehiza. It is possible that with the death of the individuals who are acquainted with the actual circumstances, Hassani's version will become the accepted version since it corresponds to the behavior patterns operative in the village.

The merging of collateral lines operates to make relations more harmonious even in those villages which appear to approach the single lineage type most closely. This village is extremely homogeneous in composition, however, and possesses no adult males who are not members of the one lineage. Its solidarity is accentuated and brought to a very high level by the falsification of genealogies. Such falsification is important in counteracting tendencies towards segmentation within lineages, but it is countered by the divisive tendencies of overcrowding and of inheritance disputes which also occur as villages become larger.

Yumbu is a stable and orderly village at the present time. The position of Shehiza is clear and uncontested. He is the only surviving male descendent of Mhandavumo, the founder of the village, and thus has clear claim over the leadership of the village and the lineage. A closely linked group has been made even closer by the amalgamation of collateral lines and village unity is at its maximum.[1] Nevertheless it is possible that a schism can develop with the death of Shehiza. It is the expectation that village leadership should devolve to the eldest son in a direct line from the deceased, but a number of complications exist in this instance which find their parallel in numbers of other villages investigated. Ramazani is Shehiza's oldest actual son, but he is younger than Rashidi, who is counted as an actual

[1] The very common occurrence of this sort of merging is discussed by Meyer Fortes in his article, 'The Structure of Unilineal Descent Groups', *American Anthropologist*, LV, No. 1 (1953), pp. 17–41.

son by everyone but Shehiza himself. Further, Shehiza favors his youngest real son, Omari, a relatively junior man, over either of the others and depends heavily upon him, so that Omari in many respects already controls the village. The men of the lineage must choose a successor when Shehiza dies, either respecting his wishes which are obviously with Omari, or over-ruling them for a more senior son who conforms to the general expectation.

Lwandai, shown in figure twelve, represents the more complex type of commoner village which I have called the multi-lineage village. Multi-lineage villages vary a great deal in their structure but most frequently are occupied by a relatively large dominant lineage and one or two attached lineages. Lwandai, which has a population of 139, is considerably less complex than many multi-lineage villages but very clearly illustrates the most common manner in which the various lineages in such a village are attached to each other. In this case all of the secondary lineages were founded through the practice of uxorilocal residence. Land was plentiful in the vicinity at the time that the founder and his two sons settled, and there has never been any attempt to reclaim land alloted to daughters whose husbands moved into the village. In fact it appears that the outsiders were viewed as a valuable source of manpower. In each case the land originally alloted to these women and their husbands was quite extensive and has been sufficient to provide fields for their descendents. Indeed, in the case of the oldest secondary lineage in the village there was sufficient land so that they have in turn given land to a daughter and her husband. This may well mark the founding of a lineage with tertiary land rights should the son of this marriage be allowed to inherit his mother's land. If he is not allowed to inherit this land he will be in a difficult, but not impossible, position. His father retains a field of about a quarter of an acre in extent near his own village of origin, and the son could return to this with the hope of obtaining another similar sized plot of land which should give him sufficient to sustain himself and his own wife and children.

At the present time only two secondary lineages are recognized as existing within the village. These two possess recognized lineage leaders, conduct their own ancestor ceremonies, and are represented in a council of adult males in the village. The other

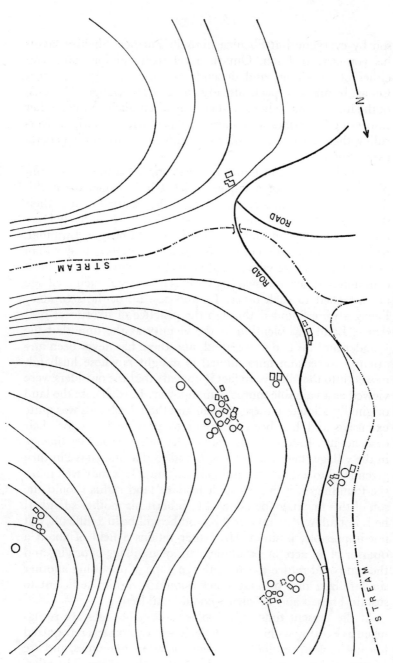

SKETCH MAP OF LWANDAI

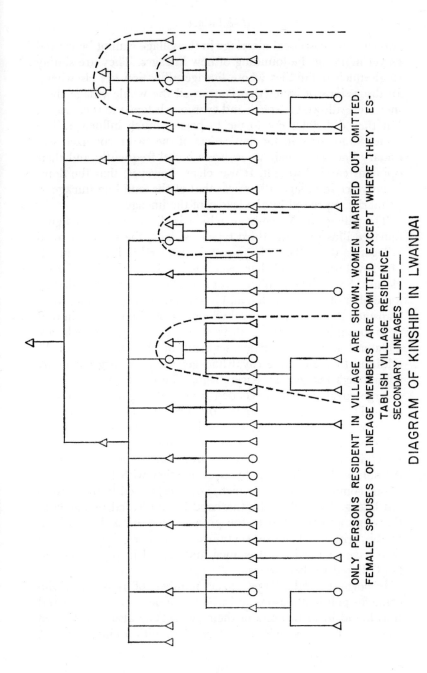

ONLY PERSONS RESIDENT IN VILLAGE ARE SHOWN. WOMEN MARRIED OUT OMITTED.
FEMALE SPOUSES OF LINEAGE MEMBERS ARE OMITTED EXCEPT WHERE THEY ES-
TABLISH VILLAGE RESIDENCE
SECONDARY LINEAGES — — —

DIAGRAM OF KINSHIP IN LWANDAI

two cases of uxorilocal marriage in the village cannot be viewed as yet marking the founding of new lineages. They are simply single nuclear families whose lineage affiliation lies elsewhere. In discussions of issues that concerned the whole village these men were allowed to speak and everyone listened to their views, but they did not seem to me to possess much influence. The same cannot be said for the leaders of the two recognized secondary lineages. Their voices were heard frequently and their opinions carried weight. It was clear, however, that the dominant voice in village affairs was that of the founding lineage as primarily expressed by the leader of the lineage.

The village of Kwembago which is diagrammed in figure fourteen illustrates the third type of village, the *kitala*, or royal village. In this village of 275 persons leadership is in the hands of a royal lineage and there is a royal residence and burial inclosure. Kwembago, unlike most royal villages, was founded by a member of the royal clan and has a higher proportion of royal clansmen than do many royal villages. It is also unusual in that it is occupied by three distinct royal lineages which are collateral lines of a major segment of the royal clan.[1] In addition to these three royal lineages there are a great many commoners resident in Kwembago. The essential structure is a large royal lineage descended from the original settler who opened the land, portions of two other royal lineages which have close patrilineal ties with the dominant lineage but which are centered in other villages, and four commoner lineages all of which have been in the village for from two to four generations. Affinal ties link all of the lineages together with the exception of one commoner lineage which, however, is tied to the dominant lineage by a blood brotherhood bond created two generations ago and renewed in the present generation. In addition to this primary structure there are a number of isolated men who have married royal women and settled in the village on land alloted to their wives.

Important royal villages attract numbers of individuals who come for political reasons and who continue to reside there and thus found local lineages of their own. They also attract men who need land and who ally themselves with a chief and add

---

[1] I here use major segment in the sense defined by Meyer Fortes, *Dynamics of Clanship among the Tallensi* (London: Oxford University Press, 1945), p. 32.

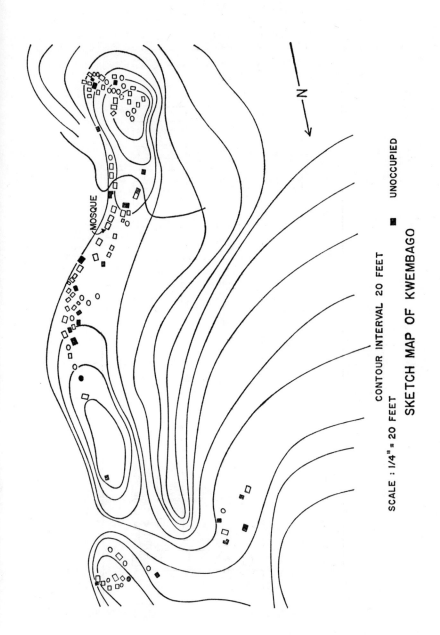

MOSQUE

CONTOUR INTERVAL 20 FEET

SCALE : 1/4" = 20 FEET

■ UNOCCUPIED

SKETCH MAP OF KWEMBAGO

N

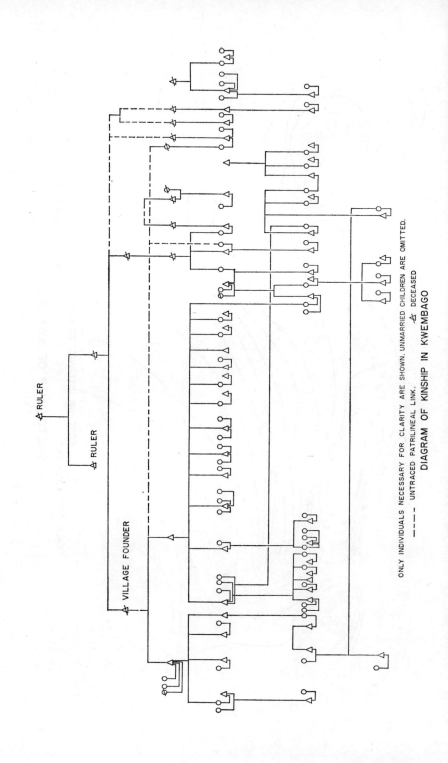

RULER

RULER

VILLAGE FOUNDER

ONLY INDIVIDUALS NECESSARY FOR CLARITY ARE SHOWN. UNMARRIED CHILDREN ARE OMITTED.
------- UNTRACED PATRILINEAL LINK.
DECEASED

DIAGRAM OF KINSHIP IN KWEMBAGO

to his power in return for his economic aid and protection. It is very frequently the case that men with political aspirations or men who hold the position of councillor or messenger to a chief will attempt to marry a woman in the chief's village and secure lands and a house for her there. This is done for a number of reasons not the least of which is convenience. Long debates, court cases, and other such affairs may take up a great deal of time and it's far easier to have a house at the *kitala* village than to return on foot several miles to one's own village in the dark. Furthermore, a great deal of informal gossip and talk floats around a chief's village and it is useful to be in a position to hear it. Since it is also very helpful to secure as many ties as possible to the chief whom one serves, marriage within his lineage looms important for the politically ambitious.

Marriage into a chief's lineage is one way of acquiring a residence within a new village but it is not the only way. Settlement within a new village is not casual, however, and it is not usually accomplished without some previous tie in the village. Outsiders are acceptable if there is land available but not without a sponsor who is in a position to guarantee the new settler's good behavior. Once a man is established in a village, he may be in a position to intercede for his own close agnatic kin should they wish to follow him. Thus brother often follows brother into a chief's village in a pattern beneficial to all. The new settlers gain land from the move while the chief gains followers with strong obligations to him.

Mother's brother-sister's son ties may also provide the connection necessary for settlement in a new village. Relations with mother's brother are quite close. In times of stress support is frequently sought not only from one's lineage mates but from one's mother's brother as well. Indeed it is frequently said: 'Have you no *mtumba* (mother's brother)? Then you must fend for yourself.' Mutual help, visiting, attendance at ancestor rituals, and economic exchanges are fairly frequent between sister's son and mother's brother and establish connections which may lead to a move into mother's brother's village should land be abundant there and scarce at home or should relations with one's father become strained. There are a number of such situations in Kwembago most of which probably mark permanent settlement, for it is usually only grave misunderstandings which prompt a mother's brother to demand the return of land from a sister's son.

The complex ties which unite a village like Kwembago are further elaborated through the creation of quasi-kinship ties produced by blood brotherhood. The recognition of blood brotherhood (called *mbuya* or *amini*) is very common. Entrance into such bonds is even extended to men of other tribes and may be widely ramified in the case of an important man. Such ties constitute a considerable source of support, for the obligations created are like those of brothers but are said to be even more dependable. The troubles between brothers are the subject of numerous proverbs which would seem to indicate that the Shambala view the relationship as important but difficult. Thus, 'All the brothers of a father won't get along with each other,' or, 'Ten fruits on a stem; there are rotten ones,' are proverbs that everyone knows and can explain, particularly with reference to quarrels over inheritance or supposed favoritism displayed by a father which causes jealousy. The institution of blood brotherhood is explicitly viewed as a support against the perfidy of real brothers. It was explained in the following terms when I entered such a pact:

> Your *amini* is better than your brother. *Amini* should share everything and never treat each other badly or a curse will follow them until they die from it. Your brother can quarrel with you over the division of property, and he may try to eat your share, but your *amini* will not do such things to you. A man who walks with *amini* cannot lose the way.

At least one lineage within Kwembago is present solely through the bonds of blood brotherhood established two generations ago between its founder and the head of the principal royal lineage in the village. Besides this, two men married to daughters of the present head of the dominant lineage and resident in the village are sons of blood brothers of this lineage leader. Undoubtedly other such links exist in the village which did not come to light in my investigation.

Kinship or quasi-kinship are important means of relating the individual within the authority structure of a village but there are other important means within a royal village like Kwembago. Such villages are the center of ritual and political power for large regions. Service to the chief as a councillor, guard, ritual functionary, and the like establishes position in the village. In former times the village would have contained a substantial number of slaves owned by the chief himself or other powerful men of the royal clan or of the council.

Kinship, political subordination, and, finally, rights in land act to define the locus of authority within the village. The position of the royal clan is periodically reinforced by the observation of rites of royal ancestor worship which reiterate the sacredness of the relation between the lineage and the land. Beyond this, certain functionaries in royal ancestor worship are drawn from the commoner clans and the political and ritual affiliation of commoners to the royal clan is thus maintained. Mourning ceremonies, weddings, and the obligations between affines and maternal kinsmen all reinforce the daily face-to-face contact of villagers and underscore the unity of common residence.

Chapter V

THE ROYAL CHARTER

IN the introduction the hypothesis was put forward that the traditions of the arrival of the founder and the genealogies associated with it offer a charter for the authority of the royal clan and also provide the channels of authority within the Shambala state. Traditional and supernatural elements are woven together into a complex of stories and beliefs which act as a charter for the *status quo* of Shambala society. The most outstanding part of this charter is the story of Mbega, a migration story recounting the coming of the founder of the royal clan. This may be viewed as a key element in the ideology of the Shambala state, for it recounts the founding, the elaboration of the structure, the marvelous deeds which made the founder powerful and 'good', and the special powers inherited by this founder's sons. Major additions may be made to the Mbega tale itself by collecting the traditions of other clans which elaborate on the particulars of their relation to the royal clan. The whole of the complex in all of its detail clearly acts to validate contemporary arrangements and provides the people with a satisfying and orderly account of their relations to their neighbors.

Whether or not it is true in an historical sense, nearly all commoners claim that their ancestors voluntarily asked for chiefs, and, similarly, chiefs do not claim to rule by right of conquest but rather by invitation and right of descent. Thus the head of a commoner lineage told me about the royal village in which his lineage resided in an explanation that was repeated in essence in nearly every village in which I worked.

My father's father and his brothers started going to the *kitala* of Shekiniashi because he saw their cases and settled the disputes so that none were angry and there was an end to trouble. They took him sheep for that and they said to him, 'Send your son so that he can hear our disputes and learn them well and we will keep him in our place and give him sheep and cattle to hear our

76

cases.' Since then the sons of Shekiniashi have lived here and helped *Mdoe* and the others.

Such an attitude seems to me to be of crucial importance to the stability and enduring qualities of the state for it implies that the powers of the elite are conceived as legitimate and the system is viewed as in some sense beneficial to all. This does not mean that chiefs are not sometimes feared or that their actions are not sometimes oppressive. The power of chiefship involves the right of coercion, and many chiefs have been feared. Members of the royal clan are often likened to leopards, and it is said that they tear the people apart and eat them. However, approval of the legitimate exercise of coercion within the system is general, regardless of the personal disapproval of some one individual who may overzealously exercise his authority.

It is useful to examine the significance of the charter from two different viewpoints. On the one hand, it can be seen as the means by which the chief legitimizes his claim to position. Through the elaborate tracing of genealogy he is able to justify his occupation of a position and his exercise of power. At the same time, however, the commoner is equally concerned with the traditions since they serve to establish the guide lines for chiefly action. There is a certain fluid quality to the chief-commoner relation which comes clearly out of these two ways of viewing the charter. The commoners are concerned with the limitation of the power of the chief and with those aspects of the tradition which emphasize the notion that the chief holds his position at the sufferance of the people through their voluntary acceptance of him as arbitrator and focus for certain super-natural powers. The chief is concerned more with the justification for exercise of power and for the extension of such power on an ever broadening basis. It is not the question shall chiefs exist which concerns anyone, but rather to what extent shall the chief exercise coercive authority?

The essence of political relations I take to be the control and exercise of legitimate coercion. Physical coercion is a universal of human relations which has several aspects. The long maturation period of humans produces a kind of subordination which depends at first upon simple physiological immaturity. As time passes, such subordination is transformed increasingly into

77

cultural terms. The child learns the values which can be conveyed by words and precepts as it learns to speak and to observe. Familial authority and the values inculcated within the family are, for the child, absolute. 'The home is the world of the child, and it is a governed world . . . He is taught that this is right and that is wrong . . . this is good and that is bad; this is honorable and that is shameful. So the long process of indoctrination and habituation begins . . . There is no alternative and there is no appeal. It (authority) may be disobeyed, but that is evasion. It may be defied, but that is rebellion. Here the authority is absolute. No other is even conceivable. . . . The world of the child is a closed world of absolute authority, mitigated by affection.' [1] The corporate lineage is characterized by the extension of such relations to the limits of the lineage. Familial authority is political in the sense that it is the vehicle for carrying out the political functions of maintaining internal order and external defense, for the corporate lineage exists within a field of corporate lineages. Within a great class of societies such as acephalous segmentary societies there may be no legitimate coercion beyond the lineage. Physical coercion occurs in the form of violent self-help or the blood feud, but it may be regarded as illegitimate.

Within Shambala society, however, chiefship provides the vehicle for the exercise of legitimate coercion beyond the corporate lineage. Such coercion may reach inside the corporate lineage but most frequently deals with lineages as units. Authority within lineages is based upon values which are inculcated within the family and extend out to the total lineage. The authority of chiefship, of a sacred or charismatic type, extends downwards to the heads of lineages and makes of these lineage heads the meeting point of these two types of authority system. [2] These two sets of values are powerfully bound together through

[1] R. M. MacIver, *The Web of Government* (New York: The Macmillan Company, 1947), p. 29.
[2] Max Weber, *The Theory of Social and Economic Organization*, translated by A. M. Henderson and Talcott Parsons (Glencoe: The Free Press and the Falcon's Wing Press, 1947), pp. 358–73. Weber here discusses the concept of charisma and its routinization and suggests several modes of routinization including that which arises through the conception that charisma is a quality transmitted by heredity. He notes that it is sometimes necessary to select the proper heir within the kinship group, for example, by certain qualities or marks or by contests among the heirs. Both of these attributes appear to be present within the Shambala state.

the symbolic identification of chiefs and subjects as expressed in the public rituals of the chief and the participation of subjects in these. The proverb, 'The chief is the people', is not simply an aphorism but the expression of a central political theory, which clearly recognizes that there can be no chief without subjects. Beyond this, the two sets of values are also linked by the expression of the relations among chiefs in kinship terms.

The Mbega Tradition

The Mbega tradition is known to nearly everyone and is recounted with obvious pride, while disparaging remarks are made about neighboring people who lack such traditions. Most versions of the tradition are simple and brief and contain only the essential outline of the founding of the state and the qualities of the hero, Mbega. However, some old men who have spent their lives as councillors or chiefs and who have used the tradition as the basis for decisions in war and legal disputes have extremely detailed versions to tell. The detail has been preserved in print through the efforts of Abdallah Bin Hemed Bin Ali Liajjemi, an Arab who collected much of it before the turn of the century and recorded it in fine literary Swahili.[1] His version was published in three parts over a four-year period,[2] part one of which was thought to have passed completely out of existence until the recent discovery of a manuscript copy from which a reprint has now been made.[3] Parts two and three of this original edition are very rare but a few may still be found, and the manuscripts of both of these volumes are in the possession of the library of the School of Oriental Studies in London.

This early version contains much more detail than I was able to obtain, but all of the versions agree in substance. It is perhaps useful to recapitulate the story for its utility in clarifying the relations between kinship and political organization as conceived by the Shambala.

The account begins in the Nguu Hills, an area of low hills

[1] Roland Allen, 'The Story of Mbega', *Tanganyika Notes and Records*, No. 1 (1936), p. 38.

[2] Abdallah Bin Hemed Bin Ali Liajjemi, *Habari Za Wakilindi* (Sehemu ya kwanza, Sehemu ya pili, Sehemu ya tatu), (Msalabani: U.M.C.A. Press, 1901-5).

[3] Abdallah Bin Hemed Bin Ali Liajjemi, 'Habari Za Wakilindi' (Sehemu ya kwanza), *The Journal of the East African Swahili Committee*, No. 27 (1957).

and dry bush country not far to the south of the Usambara Mountains, which is now occupied by the Zigua, who are closely related in language and culture to the Shambala. The hero, Mbega, became involved in a dispute with his kin over inheritance and determined to leave his home country. There follows an account of wanderings, pig hunting, wonderful hunting magic practiced by Mbega, and his brave deeds. In some versions he is accompanied by some boon companions; in some his sister or sisters also accompany him. In all versions he hunts pigs and makes friends of people in the territories where he wanders by killing these marauders of the fields and distributing their meat. He settles once at a place called Kilindi, but the son of a chief who has befriended him is killed in a hunting accident and he flees with some companions to escape the wrath of the chief. During this part of his life he acquires a packet of magic which allows the control of clouds and of the rain, as well as control over animals and means of foretelling some future events.

It is after fleeing from the consequences of the hunting accident that Mbega and his companions first come to the Usambara Mountains. In almost all versions, Mbega is said to have been invited to the Usambaras by the people of Zirai, a village on the southern escarpment above the plains. These people saw the smoke of his campfires and went to investigate. After finding that he hunted pigs, they invited him to their village to rid them of pigs that ate the crops. He became locally celebrated while living at Zirai and was invited to move to the village of Bumbuli, which was a larger and more powerful place. While at Bumbuli he became very well known and attracted a large following of young men who hunted with him and who listened to his many stories of marvelous adventures. Finally, a delegation from the village of Vuga was sent by the headman Tuli to invite him to come help them rid the country of pigs.[1] He agreed to this and left for Vuga. During this journey through the forest he killed a lion (in some versions a buffalo) with a club. This incident is considered very significant since it

[1] The hunting and eating of pigs seems a curious element, particularly since the majority of Shambala are now Moslems. However, it is stressed in all versions of the story and it is certainly the case that villages near the remanent rain forests suffer considerable crop damage from wild pigs. Hunts are sometimes organized to cut down such damage but the pigs are not eaten by most people.

proved he was powerful and fearless.[1] It is supposedly incorporated in a praise greeting which was directed to Mbega who was saluted *Simbamwene* (Meaning very doubtful,—enye or mwene is an adverb indicating state or condition of. It probably means Lionlike) to which he replied, Mmmmmmm (or sometimes, Eeeeee). This greeting is still used for the paramount chief and is also his formal title of office.

At Vuga, Mbega not only hunted but was asked to arbitrate disputes and to help in the councils. He was so successful that his power was soon greater than the power of the council and of Tuli, the headman. While Mbega was staying at Bumbuli he had married and not long after coming to Vuga his young wife had a son whom he named Buge. The people of Bumbuli determined to get the son back to Bumbuli, saying that he should be known to his kinsmen or otherwise Bumbuli would be as nothing compared to Vuga. A delegation was sent to Vuga to request that Buge be allowed to live at Bumbuli. Mbega agreed to this and so Buge went to live with his mother's people in Bumbuli. Not only was he reared at Bumbuli but the elders conceived a plan whereby a wise man was appointed by Mbega to live with the boy and to train him in the art of hearing cases and settling disputes. He sat with the elders at all cases and was given a beast at every judgment which called for the forfeiture of cattle. When Buge was in his middle teens, the elders of Bumbuli asked that he be appointed Mbega's representative in their country. This was done and messengers were appointed to maintain contact between Mbega in Vuga and the new chief in Bumbuli.

The tradition goes on to tell how the men of Ubiri (a large village to the north of Vuga) had meanwhile grown fearful and jealous of the growing power of Bumbuli and were also anxious to benefit from the wisdom of Mbega. They wished to gain peace and wealth that Mbega was able to bring so they conceived a plot in which Mbega was invited to their village, entertained, and finally allowed to see the most beautiful girl in Ubiri. After he had admired her, he was asked if he would like her as a wife. He agreed to this and she bore him a son whom he named Kimweri. The men of Ubiri then followed the

[1] It is stressed so heavily that I am inclined to think there must be other meanings, but I could gain no satisfactory explanation of them.

lead of Bumbuli and had the young child come to Ubiri to live, thus planning to get a chief whose power would rival that of Buge at Bumbuli. The plan did not work as they had hoped for various reasons, the details of which cannot concern us here. However, the pattern was now established: the means for gaining peace and well-being as well as power, was clearly through the acceptance of a son of Mbega.

The traditions go on to tell of the long, prosperous chiefship of Mbega, and of Buge's rule in Bumbuli. Mbega's death is recounted and his transfer of his powerful secrets to his son Buge is related in detail. Buge was then chosen to succeed his father in Vuga, although secretly at first to keep a succession war from starting, as the other sons were regarded as potential trouble points. The country which was united at this time comprised a large area on the south side of the mountains including the regions under the control of the three large villages of Vuga, Bumbuli, and Ubiri.

During the reign of Buge, most of the northern side of the mountains sent wives to Buge in order to join in the benefits of peace and the reduction of intervillage fighting. Buge opened many paths through the mountains and brought good times, but his rule was cut short by an early death. His son Shebuge was chosen to fill his place and, unlike his father and grandfather, was very warlike. He conquered widely and extended the rule of the chiefs of Vuga to all of the mountains and a great deal of the surrounding plains. He finally met his death in Zigua country while trying to annex the country from which his grandfather was said to have come. The elders chose Shebuge's son Kimweri as chief at the news of Shebuge's death, and Kimweri embarked on a career of consolidation. Kimweri sent his brothers and sons and even some daughters to act as chiefs throughout the sprawling territory now acknowledging loyalty to Vuga.

The Mbega Tradition and the Stance of the Chief

According to the Mbega tradition and the local traditions of other clans as well, the whole of the Usambaras was divided into small village communities without overall coordination before the spread of the royal clan. There is good reason to assume that some of the spread of the royal clan was accomplished by force; indeed the traditions affirm that this was the case. However, much of it is claimed to have been peaceful and is linked to the personal and supernatural qualities of Mbega and of his descendents. Thus Mbega is attributed with control over rain and it is believed that this power may be inherited by his descendents. At the present time a chief who is thought to possess such power is rewarded by gifts at the end of any unseasonable drought.

Not all chiefs are considered to have inherited this, however, and it is not held to be the only attribute which makes the royal clan powerful or desirable. According to Shambala views of personality, not all men possess the foresight and sensitivity necessary for successful and peaceful dealings with other men. Some are impatient and inclined to use force as a means of dealing with other men. Recourse to force and intimidation may make a man important, or a person to reckon with, but it does not make him desirable in the eyes of the Shambala. It is better to talk things out and to use persuasion and discussion. Indeed, even passive stubborness is to be preferred to outright confrontation. 'A good chief is one who will walk with the people,' is a frequently quoted proverb. One has the impression that most chiefs have heard it until they are sick of it, but they nevertheless respect it and operate in terms of it much of the time. This attribute is ascribed to Mbega and is thought to be inherited within the royal clan. However, it is sometimes lacking in chiefs, but then it cannot be expected that every man will inherit all the desirable qualities of his ancestors. Old men tell stories their fathers told them of the patience of Kimweri *zanyumbai*. Even this great chief's name is supposed to come from his willingness to listen. *Zanyumbai* means 'of the house' and is supposed to refer to his unwillingness to leave his house as an old man when he had the wisdom to see that he should always be ready to hear a case. Hot-bloodedness in chiefs is exciting but dangerous. I was nearly speared in a mock skirmish between two excited men who must have been in their seventies, who were describing the wars of a chief named Shewale. They got their spears from the house, danced and feinted until one accidentally hit the other. They concluded by sitting down and saying, 'But he was a bad chief, too sharp.'

Like rain making, the attributes of patience and astute judgment of the desires of others are considered to be largely a matter beyond the control of the individual. It is recognized that age brings patience and judgment to a certain degree, but an old man can be as foolish and hot-headed as a youth of twenty, although probably not as often. At any rate, sensitivity to the nuances of others' opinion and the careful settlement of differences without recourse to coercion is a highly valued trait which is ascribed to all of the really great Kilindi chiefs. This stance is valued only within the context of Shambala society, however. Aggressiveness and war making are not without utility provided they are directed outward. Thus apparently conflicting statements appear in traditional history which depict a man as gentle and patient in his dealings with his subjects and also as a ferocious warrior and slaver. It appears to me that these two things are simply regarded as appropriate to different contexts, and it is the man who carries behavior over from one of these contexts to the other who is regarded as undesirable.

It is perhaps in this light that elaborate purification rites following warfare may be most profitably regarded. Such rites last for more than a week following fighting and entail shaving the head, bathing, and observing sexual continence. If one has killed an enemy the rites are much more prolonged and elaborate and last for two or more months. I view these as signaling the transition from one mode of behavior to the other. What one is being cleansed of is the dangerous supernatural pollution of war, but it is also being driven home that the warfare is over and that the individual should divest himself of the attitudes appropriate to fighting.[1] Chiefs, in fact, should not themselves engage directly in warfare but should remain behind, delegating leadership in war to others. One informant, upon explaining this to me, remarked, 'It eats the chiefship for a chief to kill a man himself or to be angry.'

Thus not only are chiefs viewed as rain makers but are thought also to have certain innate attributes of personality which fit them for office. Indeed, as has been suggested, there

---

[1] I am indebted in this view to many discussions with Dr. Fred Gearing and to his notion of 'structural pose'. See Fred Gearing, 'The Structural Poses of 18th Century Cherokee Villages', *American Anthropologist*, Vol. 60, No. 6, Part 1 (1958), pp. 1148–57.

are certain aspects of ritual and political structure which make
the role of chief as an arbitrator and talker easier to assume
since direct violent action is expressly avoided in the chiefs'
role.

Whatever the historical significance of the Mbega story, and
corroboration of parts of it by early European investigators
makes it appear to have some substance, its sociological significance is great. It stands as a strong social device defining the
proper role behavior of the chief and at the same time defining
the behavior of others toward the chief. This function of the
Mbega story seems to me to emerge clearly from the use to
which it is put during the installation of a chief. The selection
of a chief is complex and will be discussed later. Here I am
concerned only with the manner in which the chief takes office.
At this time there is considerable public ceremonial in which
all of the adult males of the chiefdom participate. The crucial
part of the installation is the point at which the chief is charged
with his duties (called *Kumikia nkhana*) and the men swear to
support him. This ritual significantly is conducted by commoners, no member of the royal clan may install a chief. The
most important men involved are a senior councillor dispatched
by the next higher chief to indicate that chief's acceptance and
a ritual functionary called *Ngovi*. The *Ngovi* wears an elaborate
costume the most outstanding part of which is a cap of the
skin of the colobus monkey. The word *mbega* means colobus
monkey and is said to have been given to the founder of the
state after his arrival in Shambalai 'because he was so hairy'.
His real name is not known though everyone agrees it was not
mbega. The two men leading the installation remind the new
chief of the wisdom of Mbega and refer to his killing of animals
to provide food for the people and to his slaying of the lion
(or buffalo) to protect the people. They then speak of how
Mbega named his son and refer to a custom in which men
address each other '*Shebuge*' to which the reply is '*Shekulavu*',
two ritual names which alternate generationally in the Kilindi
clan but which all men may use formally as a greeting. Finally
they say 'we want you as chief if you will take care of the country
as we take care of you, as your father and your grandfather,
Mbega did'. All the men shout and raise their swords at this
point and the chief retires to the *nyumba nkuu* where he kills a

bull with which to feed everyone. A dance follows starting at the *nyumba nkuu* which is led by the *Ngovi* and which involves a kind of reenactment of Mbega's arrival in Shambalai. At this time the new chief is reminded that he cannot do his *fika* (ancestor ceremonies) without the aid of the *Ngovi*. After the dance, the new chief provides sugar-cane beer and everyone eats and drinks. The following day he is conducted through his fields by his councillors, the people clean and weed, a goat is killed in the banana fields of the chief and everyone returns to the *kitala* for more feasting. This often continues for two or three days.

The whole ceremony seems to me to be intended to stress certain aspects of the relation between chiefs and subjects. The chief is reminded of the people's voluntary acceptance of his ancestors through not only his installation by commoners but also through explicit references to how Mbega came to be a chief. He is also reminded of his duty to defend his people and to feed them if necessary. They meanwhile swear to support him, they show him his land, they do symbolic work there to indicate their support, and they eat food his wife has prepared (a sign of trust). Finally, the participation of outsiders in the chief's ancestor ritual is an indication of the public nature of these ancestors and of the mutual dependence of all the living on the royal ancestral spirits.

Royale Lineage Structure and the Chief's Position

The importance of lineage structure emerges clearly in a comparison of the royal clan with commoner clans. A distinction has been made previously between clans composed of shallow parallel lineages and clans in which the lineages are not parallel but form a deep segmentary system. It was seen that this distinction is essentially that between commoner clans and the royal clan.

It appears unlikely that this difference in clan structure can be explained simply on historical grounds. Many clans in Shambalai claim origins in the same region from which the founder of the royal clan is said to have come, yet they do not possess the type of structure which characterizes the royal clan. However, even if it were the case that the royal clan arrived in Shambalai with the type of structure it now possesses, the retention of such an atypical structure within the new society would have to be explained. Thus the functional context within which these different structures exist must be considered.

For the commoner lineage, genealogical information is of significance only with respect to settlement in a particular locale. The genealogy is utilized as a legal device for the legitimization of control over a piece of territory, as a charter for the structural relationships within the lineage, and for an explanation of the particular relationships which exist with other nearby lineages. The strong forces acting to bring about merging and telescoping tend to maintain these genealogies at a constant shallow depth in which the important information is simply reference to a first settler who opened the land.

The segmentary lineage system of the royal clan though expressed in a kinship metaphor, is an extremely important vehicle for internal political relationship. Relations among the various political groups are embedded in a genealogical framework to which the living may refer.[1] Within the royal clan itself, the broadening of the extent of political control depends heavily upon the legitimization of political power through reference to a previous royal chief. Thus the underscoring of segmentations which preceded settlement in a new location is crucial to a chief and to the lineage he founds. Not only does derivation from a previous royal lineage act to legitimize claim to chiefly position, but it also establishes the relative rank of the chief. Thus in ideal terms a descendent of some chief can attain rank equal to that of his progenitor (that is, by inheriting his position) or can become a chief at a lower rank, since any lineage he founds will necessarily be of a lower order of segmentation than the lineage from which he has split off.

In formal terms the Shambala recognize only three levels of royal chiefs. These chiefships form a ranked hierarchy of pyramidal form in which the apex is the paramount chief, whose authority is held to extend over the whole of Shambalai. Below the paramount stand a number of 'great chiefs' (pl. *wazumbe wakuu*; sing. *zumbe mkuu*) deemed accountable directly

[1] Cf. Ian Cunnison, 'History and Genealogies in a Conquest State', *American Anthropologist*, Vol. 59, No. 1 (1957), pp. 20-31, for a penetrating analysis of a similar situation in the Luapula Valley.

to the paramount and only to the paramount.[1] Under each great chief are a number of 'lesser chiefs' (pl. *wazumbe wadodo* sing. *zumbe mdodo*) accountable directly to the great chief and indirectly to the paramount.[2]

The Shambala conceptualize the system by assuming that the paramountcy is inherited by a male descendent of the ruling paramount ultimately tracing descent from the founder of the royal clan in a direct line. They view the great chiefs as holding offices established through segmentations from among the brothers of the paramount, and, finally, the lesser chiefs are seen as holding offices established through segmentations occurring within the lineages of the great chiefs. This schematic relation is shown in figure fifteen.

The real departs from these conceptions in various ways. First, although only three levels of chiefs are recognized in terms of formal position and bureaucratic authority, the gradation of social standing of chiefs is much finer and more sensitive. The lineage which holds some particular chiefship may be senior in terms of its segmentation to certain other lineages which hold chiefships of the same formal level, as can be seen in figure fifteen. In such cases the chief of the more senior lineage enjoys higher social status and is shown respect by the other more junior chiefs of the same bureaucratic level. However, the relation of all of them to the next higher bureaucratic level is theoretically identical and the more junior chiefs do not have to go through their more senior colleagues to communicate with chiefs at higher levels. This difference in social status emerges in group contexts where opinions of segmentally senior peers are given more weight or simply in any gathering where social deference is observable. I make this point primarily because it may have some effects in decision making although I was unable to detect any such result in my own investigation.

Second, succession is not so regular in fact as it is assumed to be in the ideal conceptions of the Shambala who speak as if chieftaincy always passed from father to son. The local situation may be chartered in local terms on a genealogical basis which

[1] The number of great chiefs has varied, particularly under modern administration. At present there are sixteen (1957).

[2] The number of lesser chiefs is even more variable, and figures are confusing since government recognizes some commoners as holding this rank. There are presently 158 lesser chiefs (1957).

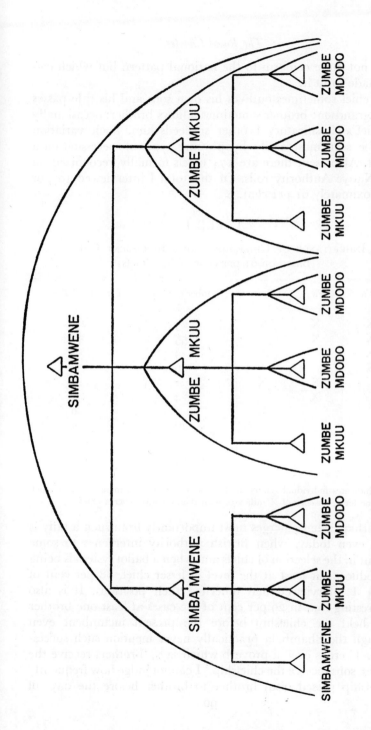

SCHEMATIC DIAGRAM OF LINEAGE RELATIONS AND RANK IN
THE ROYAL CLAN. ACTUAL SPAN AND DEPTH ARE GREATLY ABRIDGED.

SIMBAMWENE

SIMBA MWENE

ZUMBE MKUU

ZUMBE MKUU

ZUMBE MKUU

SIMBAMWENE ZUMBE MKUU

ZUMBE MDODO

ZUMBE MDODO

ZUMBE MDODO

ZUMBE MKUU

ZUMBE MKUU

ZUMBE MDODO

ZUMBE MDODO

does not quite conform to the national pattern but which can be made to fit it.

A chief sometimes outlives his own sons and his title passes to a grandson; brother sometimes follows brother; occasionally a chief's classificatory brother succeeds him. Such variation can be seen most easily by plotting types of succession on a chart. At present there are 174 chiefs formally recognized on the Native Authority rolls. Of this total I interviewed 107, or approximately 61 per cent.

TABLE I

INHERITANCE OF CHIEFSHIP AMONG INCUMBENT CHIEFS
(Based on 61 per cent of All Chiefs)

GFa.	Fa.	Bro.	Number of Cases	Per cent of Total
X	X	X	25	23
X	X		55	51
X		X	3	3
X			6	6
	X	X	1	1
	X		4	4
		X	0	0
			13	12
			107	100

X indicates individual related to the incumbent in this manner was a chief at some level, absence of X indicates such relation was never a chief.

Perhaps what emerges most importantly from such a tally is that even today, when British authority intervenes to some extent in the selection of chiefs and when a ballot system is being introduced, at least at the level of lesser chief, 88 per cent of those I interviewed had inherited their positions. It is also interesting that in 29 per cent of the cases at least one brother has held the chiefship before the present incumbent even though the Shambala practically never mention such succession. There is even a proverb which says, 'Brothers receive the wives, sons receive the chiefship.' I cannot judge how frequently chiefship passed from brother to brother before the days of

European administration, but I am sure it was not unknown, for there are references to such happenings in genealogical materials. I am not including in this the usurpations and succession wars which have taken place, for I am now concerned with succession deemed proper and possessing the sanctions of normal investiture. The absence on the chart of any cases in which the incumbent was preceded as chief by only a brother is due perhaps to the stabilization of the system under British rule. The royal clan is not extending its hegemony to new regions today and most chiefships have been held for at least two generations. The cases in which the present chief is shown as having no kin as predecessors in a chiefship are the result of diverse causes. Most of these men are commoners elevated to chiefship in recent years under the Native Authority reforms instituted by the Administration. Two cases are men of the royal clan who had great grandfathers who were chiefs but no intervening relatives because of succession wars in the royal clan.

The crucial point that emerges from examination of royal genealogical materials and the succession of incumbent chiefs is that exclusive right to a particular chiefship is held by a corporate lineage segment. It is clear that lineages of quite different depths may hold chiefships of the same rank, and it is also clear that the mode of succession to chiefship is not otherwise defined beyond a rule that the successor must be of the lineage which holds the chieftaincy, though with strong presumptive tendencies to favor a son, brother, or grandson of the chief.

The early historical accounts indicate clearly that more territory was being rapidly added to the state at the time of European contact and that this condition had existed for some period prior to contact. The character of the ruling clan is an important dynamic in such expansion. As all royal clan members consider themselves rulers, an attitude which is reinforced by most of their subjects, and as only a few hold regular and legitimate chiefship, then tension in the system gives rise to expansion in the state. In the past, unsuccessful claimants to a chieftaincy had only three courses of action available to them: they might satisfy themselves with being followers, they might agitate and attempt to usurp the chiefship, or they might leave and attempt to found a village and a chiefship elsewhere. The first course of action avoided conflict but deprived the individual of status. The second was exceedingly dangerous and often foolish or impossible when the incumbent chief was popular. The third was sometimes dangerous but was often rather easy since an incumbent chief was usually willing to help if only to get rid of a source of trouble in his village. Further, if the Mbega tradition is to be trusted at all, it appears that many villages invited chiefs of the royal clan, as in the cases of Buge and Kimweri mentioned previously. Beyond this, as the state grew large and powerful it may be assumed that it was safer to join it than to oppose it.

The Shambala state was expansive in much the same way that a segmentary society is expansive, but in this case expansion could take place even in a country that was already occupied since the royal clan imposed itself as a high status group over a pre-existing population.[1] Tension over succession appears to me to be one of the key elements in understanding the total structure of the state. It may be viewed as one of the primary factors in the expansion of the royal clan and thus of the political system. For although lineages have continued to segment through internal tension they must at the same time retain genealogical contact in order to reiterate and solidify the claim to chiefship which depends so heavily on royal derivation.

Such a system might be characterized as 'open' in the sense that chiefs appear glad to accept as subjects all those who would give them allegiance and who would acknowledge the obligations of service and conformity to the culture of the chiefs. In turn, the chief offers protection, stability, and an avenue for the settlement of disputes without recourse to feud. He also, very importantly, offers certain ritual and supernatural benefits, particularly in the matter of rain control and protection from locusts. The benefits deriving from such a system were continuously stressed by individual chiefs and commoners during

[1] C. Daryll Forde, 'The Anthropological Approach to Social Science', *The Advancement of Science*, IV, No. 15 (1947), p. 9. Forde notes that the condition for extensive proliferation of unilineal kin and the formation of large segmented clans appears to be the maintenance of social continuity over a widening series of territorial entities, a condition which requires both considerable physical mobility and facilities for continued territorial expansion. Both of these conditions were present to an outstanding degree in the Wakilindi clan.

the course of my fieldwork. The following views are representative:

> The Kilindi chiefs are good and keep the country from harm. It is not so good now that the Europeans have come and taken the *Uzumbe* (chiefship) but there are still good chiefs who help the people. We feel sad for the good times which were different from now. The maize grew and we did not fear the Masai or Teita. Everyone was afraid to trouble us because of Kimweri *za nyumbai*. People had their special ways of greeting Kimweri, as '*Mzenga welui*' (there are no fence builders). He replied, '*Boma ni Kimweri*' (I, Kimweri am a fence). Kimweri governed the people, liked them, and sometimes paid their *ng'ombe ya Ukwe* or *fulugha* (bride payments). And men sent him cattle or even little things like beer strainers or spoons or rodents to eat. He gave them sheep or goats in return. Things were good from Pangani and Tanga to Vanga. No cases troubled us and brothers were at peace because the Kilindi could see the right judgements in cases. There are some chiefs even today who know the right way in cases. Brothers will eat each other's property if there is no *zumbe* to judge for them.

Boys' and Girls' Initiation Ceremonies and the Royal Clan

I was able to collect fragmentary accounts of ceremonies for either boys or girls or both from old informants belonging to many different clans. However, in all cases except that of the Wanango clan these ceremonies have not been conducted for many years. They differ for each clan, and it must be assumed that at some time in the past each clan conducted its own initiations as well as its own rites of ancestor worship. In all cases but the Wanango to be discussed below, I was told that a long time ago people started going to the ceremonies of the Kilindi clan rather than to those which were peculiar to their own clan.

Thus an old informant named Sigi of the Wakijewaa clan asserted that he had attended the last initiation ceremonies of his clan when a young man and supplied details which put this event at about the turn of the century. Even then Sigi claimed young men had a choice and many went to the *gao*. He further stated:

> Those Wakiongwe (a clan) they used to celebrate their young men with *lukuni* (name of an initiation rite) but when they left Teita

because of hunger and came here to Tewa they went to *Zumbe's gao* because they honored him for his protection. Now they don't even remember *lukuni* but I remember even though it is not my *kolwa.* The same for Wavinakaa. That *kolwa* only honours *zumbe.* They are his people now, they have no *Wagoshi* (elders) of their own any more but they used to dance for four days and instruct their own young men. It is the same for all people now. We all go to *gao.*

It has long been held that such rites are symbolic expression of attainment of adult status and assumption of adult responsibility within a culture, and thus of full membership in that culture. It seems to me that this function is demonstrated clearly in the case at hand, where there has been the substitution of a uniform series of rites possessed by a dominant group for a greater number of differing rites practiced by smaller segments as these segments have become amalgamated with the dominant group. These ceremonies may be viewed as expressing the reality of the relation for which the Mbega myth is the charter. The acceptance of the royal ritual is a concrete display of acceptance of royal values and emulation of royal action. It is by its very nature an admission of subordination to the royal clan. At the same time, however, the integration of commoners into the body of functionaries who administer the rites may be taken as another expression of the interdependence of the two strata of Shambala society.

I shall not here deal with the form of initiation rites in any detail, for a consideration of the procedures is not central to my present task. I am concerned here only with attendance, major functionaries, and a suggestion of the significance of the rites.

Initiation may be said to begin with the ceremony for boys called *ngwaliko wa kaya.* The central part of this ceremony is the circumcision of the boy and the appointment of a mentor (*kungwi,* an initiated person) who will act as a confidant and example for the boy throughout the boy's lifetime. This *kungwi* can be of any clan and is frequently a blood brother of the boy's father. Circumcision is an individual matter and is not regulated by the chief. It is customary to circumcise boys between the ages of three and four, although a poor man sometimes puts it off until his son is ten or more. If there are several boys in a village all of about the same age, their fathers may go together

94

to meet the cost of the circumciser and the feast afterwards but this is a matter of circumstances. The total complex of ceremonies which go to make up the circumcision marks the advancement of the boy to the status of *wai*, or initiate. Boys are termed *wai* from the time of their circumcision until the termination of all initiation ceremonies and the assumption of adult status, which now usually occurs in the late teens.

There is no truly comparable circumcision ceremony for girls, although female circumcision is not uncommon in East Africa. However, women of the royal clan undergo a partial circumcision a few hours after the birth of their first child. At this time a portion of the external labiae is removed. Women who experience difficulty in conceiving sometimes have a similar operation performed if a medical practitioner advises it. In general, however, only girls of the royal clan undergo even a partial circumcision.

After the termination of the circumcision ceremonies there are no further observances until the age of puberty. When boys attain puberty, they are considered ready to undergo the central part of the initiation which is called *gao*. *Gao* is initiated by a chief or wealthy Kilindi man with a son of suitable age. This boy becomes the leader of the initiates and is termed *kiongolezi* (or, apparently in some places, *kizamu*). *Kiongolezi* must precede the other boys in all experiences connected with the *gao*. Because *gao* must be called by a member of the Kilindi clan with a boy of proper age, and because it is expensive, it is not held every year in every village, and the participants, of which there are usually twenty or more, may come from an extensive area. It is claimed that *gao* formerly lasted from three to six months but it is very much shorter at the present. Sometimes it is even combined with the circumcision, and boys of all ages are included. Many informants decried this practice and claimed that it was an attempt to economize because of the tax imposed by Government upon all dances or ceremonies. This may be a contributory reason for abridgment, but there are many other reasons including Moslem and Christian teaching, the absence of men and boys who are away working, the involvement of chiefs in Native Authority business, and the general lack of time for such long ceremonies when the money economy is becoming increasingly important. It probably also reflects the declining importance of the ritual and supernatural powers of the chief.

The term *gao* includes ceremonies for both boys and girls although the two sexes are separated and go through somewhat different experiences. However, the ceremonies are synchronized and begin with the construction of two temporary ceremonial houses called *shasha*. These are constructed under the direction of a ritual functionary called *shefaya*, who is usually a commoner and who is paid by the man who has called the initiation. He directs the *gao* for the chief because he has learned the necessary medicine to protect the ceremonies from witches, harmful magic, and dangerous spirits. The *makungwi*, or mentors of all the initiates, do the building and conduct the general ceremony. The *wai*, or initiates, spend their nights in the *shasha* during the whole of *gao* and are instructed in proper behavior by *shefaya*, *makungwi*, and any other adults who care to come. Two women play roles in the boys' initiation: the father's sister of *kiongolezi* (called *ninengazi ya gwali*, the father's sister of the initiates) and *mgundu*, who is an elderly relative of the *shefaya* and whose job it is to teach the boys proper sexual behavior. According to Cory, most of the instruction was formerly accomplished through stories or songs which were accompanied by illustrative figurines used to drive the lesson home and aid the initiates in remembering.[1] Only a few such figurines are still used in this way; most have apparently dropped completely out of use.

It appears to me to be significant, in the light of claims that all the clans formerly had their own ceremonies and that *gao* was only a Kilindi ceremony, that at present the *gao* for girls is restricted to Kilindi girls only. Girls of the commoner clans do not participate, although they do participate in a second ceremony for girls called *oza* which immediately follows *gao*. With respect to the *gao* for boys, all boys participate, Kilindi and commoner alike, although a Kilindi boy is leader of the initiates. Many variations in these ceremonies occur, although all men still must go through at least the abridged version before they may marry, become chiefs or councillors, or otherwise participate in the adult world. The same is true with regard to women. They cannot marry before participation in

[1] Hans Cory, *African Figurines* (New York: The Grove Press, 1956).

oza and a number of other rites, and in former times to conceive a child before *gao-oza* would have brought death.

The *gao* for Kilindi girls apparently does not include certain observances found in the ritual for boys. *Oza* follows, and then commoner girls begin their initiation. The bulk of the initiation ceremony for girls is not directly under the control of the chief and is the concern of the women. It does not so directly symbolize the position of the Kilindi clan as is the case with *gao*. It seems quite clear that *gao* is a Kilindi rite, for it is controlled by the Kilindi and it differs considerably from other initiation rites known in the mountains, at least as far as I could judge from the fragmentary accounts of these rites which were available to me. Furthermore, one is struck by the similarity between the rites practiced at present among the Shambala and those reported by Cory for the Nguu and Zigua.[1] If it is true, as the traditions claim, that the Kilindi clan came originally from the Nguu hills then it might be expected that such ceremonies would have been brought along and would have spread throughout the mountains as the Kilindi clan underwent expansion.

It is often the case that a negative instance serves well to substantiate a limited hypothesis, and such seems to be the case with the view here advanced that *gao* is meant to symbolize acceptance of the royal clan. At the present time, only one commoner clan, the Wanango (sing. Mnango) still retains its own ceremonies for boys. Within this clan the individual is given the choice of attending the ceremonies of his own clan (called *mshitu*) or those of the chief (*gao*). Attendance at *gao* excludes the possibility of attending the *mshitu*. The individual is told that he must make this choice, and it is made quite explicit that he is Mnango first and foremost if he attends the Wanango ceremony. If he chooses to go to the ceremony of the chief he is Shambala and only secondarily Mnango.

It is significant in this light that the Wanango clan possesses an organization somewhat like that of the Kilindi clan. It is composed of a series of segmentary levels, genealogies are long and detailed and act to articulate closely the lineages of which the clan is composed, and there is a certain amount of coordination of activities within the total clan. This is particularly the

[1] *Ibid.*

case with respect to initiation ceremonies and ancestor worship. The total clan does not act as a body to carry out the initiation ceremonies but the timing of ceremonies is coordinated in that all localized lineages follow the lead of the lineages in the vicinity of the village of Shume, which is held to be the *tongo*, or site of original settlement of the clan. Further, one lineage leader in the clan is *primus inter pares*, and other lineage heads defer to his lead with respect to ancestor worship and initiation ceremonies.

The Wanango claim independence from Kilindi chieftaincy in a number of ways and are fond of telling the history of their relations with the Kilindi. The following is frequently told:

> We Wanango were here in the country before Mbega and we were many. We came long ago from Upare and stayed at Shume. Many *Wagoshi* (elders) led the people there at Shume and there was one, Mbogo, there when Mbega came to the Wakinatuli at Vuga. At that time Wanango were quarreling, some wanted Mbogo and others didn't because he ate many cattle and always came to the people for more. Now Mbogo was a big drinker of honey wine and so some Wanango made much wine and invited him and also three of Tuli's men from Vuga because Mbogo was a great warrior. When he had drunk much wine those men killed him. Then they sent the *Mlinga* (a magical headdress) to Vuga and gave it to Mbega. Now *Mlinga* has power so that when you wear it no one can refuse your command. It was we ourselves who killed Mbogo along with Wakinatuli and we chose Mbega and gave him power. We gave him his wife too. We are *Tumba* (mother's brothers) to the Wakilindi. Mbega and after him his sons have learned from us as all men must learn from *Mtumba*. Not all the Wanango wanted Mbega or even his son and it wasn't until Kimweri *zanyumbai* that we all took the Wakilindi as our chiefs. Even now we are as great as they and follow because our fathers swore the oath and because the Wakilindi have taken our ceremonies for their own.

While the Wanango defer to the Kilindi it is significant to our analysis that they also claim a special connection as 'mother's brothers' to the Kilindi clan. This is not always acknowledged by members of the Kilindi clan but it usually is in those regions where the Wanango are numerous. As we have seen, the Wanango have a tradition which holds that the wife of Mbega was a Wanango girl and that the Wanango thus were mother's brothers to Mbega's son and therefore to all Kilindi. This tradition regulates behavior between Wanango and Kilindi rather importantly, and I have frequently heard Kilindi chiefs appeal to Wanango councillors or litigants with the term *mtumba* (mother's brother). Many Kilindi deny this relation, but enough accept it so that I encountered it with considerable frequency.

The Wanango quite explicitly view their retention of their own ceremony for boys as at least a partial reservation about the position of the royal Kilindi clan but at the same time they accept this position in other ways through their claim to being mother's brothers to the Kilindi and through a host of traditions which hold that much Kilindi ritual and belief is really Wanango belief borrowed by the Kilindi. Whether this is in fact true or not cannot be said since it is beyond the reach of historical documentation, but the belief is of great importance since it is on this basis that the Wanango explain their acceptance of the whole state organization. The very facts which make the Wanango stand out as a large and rather more highly organized commoner clan at the same time point up the position of the Kilindi clan with relation to other segments of the society. It is the ideology of superior status and born fitness to rule which characterizes the Kilindi as a royal clan, and it is the acceptance of this ideology through the concrete acts of ancestor worship, initiation ceremonies, and reference to tradition which binds the commoners to the chiefs and chiefly lineages.

Chapter VI

SYSTEMS OF AUTHORITY

IN our discussion of lineages, it has been suggested that those lineages which possess a name and a territory and which we have termed 'minimum effective lineages' have political significance. Such lineages are viewed as corporate groups which may have relations with other corporate entities and they further possess a leader through whom such relations are normally conducted. It is true that all members of a minimum effective lineage are viewed, and view themselves, as responsible for each other's actions; however any dealings between a lineage and the outside should properly involve the lineage head. Since such a minimum effective lineage comprises a village or a segment of a village, the lineage head is *ipso facto* a village headman or at the very least a ward or neighborhood head man. The head of the senior lineage in a large multilineage commoner village is a man of considerable importance controlling as he does perhaps fifty or more adult males and is a power to be reckoned with.[1] Men of such standing are more powerful and important than are those men of royal rank who are far removed from succession to a chiefship and whose status is very similar to that of commoners.

The status of a commoner lineage head may be differentiated from the status of a royal chief, however. The contrast may be stated in terms of a separation between authority based upon kin relations, that is the exercise of authority within a familial situation, and that specialized authority vested in the institution of chiefship which is expressly political in nature. There is certainly a difference to be discerned in the exercise of authority within a nuclear or compound family, and the exercise of

---

[1] It will be recalled that seniority in a commoner village is defined by prior occupation and control over land. Junior lineages are secondary or tertiary holders in land rights who were allowed settlement in the first place through their expressed willingness to recognize the authority of the prior occupants.

authority within a total lineage. The first is clearly a group based upon face to face relationship while the latter is characterized by the extension of such individual roles to collectivities, but nevertheless in both it is the fact of kinship which defines the nature and quality of the authority. Chiefship on the other hand, derives from shared understandings about the exercise of legitimate coercion in those classes of relations which are not based upon kinship.

In the past, cursing was the ultimate sanction for familial authority. The curse, called *ute wa tate* (the curse of my father), could be uttered by an individual family head or by the head of a lineage and in either case was a terrible measure, for the victim of a father's curse could expect every kind of trouble relieved only by eventual death. The wording of such curses seems to have varied but was approximately as follows, 'My son, if you are not my son may you be happy in the world, if you are, may you have difficulties.' Such a curse needed no witnesses, no manipulation of objects, nor any other special actions and once uttered could not be retracted. Less severe but nevertheless still very grave sanctions were expulsion from the family or lineage, the withholding of ancestor ceremonies and physical beating. The last appears to have been rare in the past and is certainly not frequent today. However expulsion and refusal to do ancestor ceremonies have lost some of their force and physical beating is sometimes resorted to in their stead. The curse is still greatly feared but is so severe as to be resorted to only rarely. Cases are cited with awe as was the following:

In 1918 at the *Kitala* of Bumbuli a man named Kilozo brought a case against his brother's son which accused the young man of practicing sorcery. The brother's son denied this and swore on his own blood before the elders that he was not a sorcerer. If he lied he would die from his oath but many days passed and he did not. Now he came to court and the elders saw that he still lived so they told Kilozo to pay a goat to have his son's head shaved to end the oath. Kilozo paid and the case was ended but he still felt doubt in his heart and he consulted with a diviner to find if the oath was proper and the signs showed it was not, so Kilozo cursed his brother's son. Only two months later the son's wife who was pregnant died and after that mourning was over, his son died, and the other men of his family died until all of them were dead. Curses like this are very strong and we Shambala fear to use them. Kilozo was very headstrong and was too angry. The curse will follow you and it can't be broken.

Disinheritance or the withholding of marriage wealth is often attempted and may be effective, but a young man can often force his father's hand in such an affair by appeal to his grandfather or to the lineage as a whole. The provision of marriage wealth is a moral obligation and even when a father has provocation he is hard put to justify such an action unless the offences of a son have been so grave as to merit expulsion from the lineage and loss of all rights as a lineage member. Usually such is not the case and it is simply wilful disobedience on the part of the son which has provoked a father into denial of property. It is a delaying action but not a powerful punishment.

Life and death are rarely within the range of familial power although in former times a father had the legitimate power to kill his newborn children. Since it was the normal procedure for the wife to go to her father's house for the birth of a child, the father did not usually see the baby for some time after birth. In the past it might be as much as several weeks before he visited his wife and viewed the child. Nevertheless he could put it to death in case of various deformities. However, this was most frequently done by those old women who aided the mother during birth and was usually done in cases of multiple births or breach births. A father had the power, indeed was expected, to kill a child who cut its top teeth first and apparently albinos were sometimes killed by their fathers. A man also had the right to decide whether children conceived in adultery by his wives or born out of wedlock by his daughters might live. These considerations notwithstanding, it is public opinion and the ultimate sanction of the curse which constitute the major part of familial authority and the subordination of junior generations.

The authority of a lineage head rests on bases other than familial ties only in those cases of multilineage villages where a second lineage exists which is subordinate in terms of the decision-making process within the village because of its secondary right to land. Even in cases of this sort, there are often so many ties of affinity and filiation between the two lineages that dealings take on the nature of kin relations. As was suggested in the section dealing with village form, movement into a new village is usually predicated on some sort of kin tie within the village. It appears that this is so precisely because it is in these terms that a lone individual may be integrated into the authority system which exists within the village. A mother's brother-sister's son relation, a marriage, a blood brotherhood tie, all of these allow the flow of authority in kinship terms.

Chiefly Authority

A distinction has been made between two types of authority within Shambala society. There is that authority which we may call familial and which is exercised within recognized kinship groupings, and there is the authority of chiefship which extends to all members of the society. Chiefly authority may be seen to operate to a large extent beyond the kin group. It may, but rarely does, reach inside the family or the lineage. It primarily treats of lineages as groups which have relations with each other and with the chief. In interlineage relations the chief is characterized as monopolizing the exercise of authority. The acceptance of this monopoly is in the first place based upon a shared tradition of charisma. Mbega, the royal founder, is portrayed in terms which conform closely to Weber's description of the charismatic leader. As Weber put it, 'in primitive circumstances this peculiar kind of deference is paid to prophets, to people with a reputation for therapeutic or legal wisdom, to leaders in the hunt and heroes in war'.[1] The acceptance of his descendants is based upon their inheritance of these qualities. This recognition of the inheritance of charisma leads not only to the acceptance of each particular royal chief but has a further implication. The growth of the lineage of the magical leader leads eventually to segmentation. The new lineages thus founded also eventually segment and so on. Since chiefs are bound together within this continually segmenting system, the acceptance of such a chief means the acceptance of the whole

---

[1] Max Weber, *The Theory of Social and Economic Organization*, translated by A. M. Henderson and Talcott Parsons (Glencoe: The Free Press and The Falcon's Wing Press, 1947), p. 359.

system of chiefs. Thus there is a division in the society between a body of rulers and a body of ruled. This cleavage is further reinforced by the differential in wealth which results from tribute, fines, and the right to service which the chief may legitimately claim.

Within a system of this type the source of power of each royal authority is essentially the same. Each chief, through inheritance, participates directly in the charisma of the founder. A royal chief does not exercise power delegated by the paramount and limited by the over-riding and essentially different powers of this supreme authority; rather, he exercises the same powers and possesses the same rights limited only by the lesser number of his people and his familial subordination to the heads of greater lineage segments in the royal clan.

The familial authority system is of great importance in the Shambala political order not only because the relations among chiefs are largely structured in this way but also because kinship groups, primarily the corporate lineage, retain a considerable responsibility for the security of the individual and the regulation of social relationships. There is always the latent possibility of recourse to self-help in any dispute which occurs. If a dispute occurs within a corporate lineage, it is the legitimate business of the lineage to settle it and a chief would not normally interfere unless invited to do so by the lineage except in cases of homicide or witchcraft. On the other hand, interlineage relations are the points of discontinuity in a segmentary system and it is here that the chief claims a monopoly upon the exercise of force. Any attempt to resort to self-help in the settlement of interlineage disputes must be immediately challenged by the chief who undertakes to settle such disputes through the exaction of compensation and the application of fines.

Homicide and violence among lineages calls the chief's power into action, for he must fix blame, exact compensation, levy fines and guarantee the settlement. It is difficult to know at present whether delicts frequently resulted in violent self-help in pre-contact times, but it is quite clear that the chief was concerned that such challenges to his authority were quelled. Informants were unanimous in claiming that murder or assault was immediately referred to the chief with which the injured party was affiliated. Thus when questioning a very elderly

informant named Bege with respect to the murder of one of his
brothers which occurred about 1915 I was told the following:

> We had drunk much *woki* (honey beer) when there was a fight
> between my elder brother and a man from Mngaro and that man
> killed my brother and then he ran off into the bush. We all
> searched for him but we could not find him so we sent a message
> to the *zumbe* of Mngaro and another message to the *kitala* at
> Mlalo. The *zumbe* of Mngaro found that man at the house of his
> wife in another village where his mother's brother was and they
> brought him to the *kitala* where the old men heard our case and
> the *zumbe mkuu* told him he must pay the cattle to my *chengo*.

When I asked if they would have killed the murderer if they had
caught him all the loungers who were listening to my discussion
with Bege laughed and Bege pretended not to have heard. I
persisted with questioning on this line and eventually Bege
became quite irritated at my ignorance and explained that
chiefs were great men in the old days and they did not allow
wanton killing and war among lineages. 'It eats the chiefship
for common people to do the things that only a chief can do.
It is like the District Commissioner who is angry when a case
is hidden from him.'

The action which a chief took in such cases seems designed
to emphasize the point that murder is an injury to the body
politic and a challenge to the authority of the chief rather than
a private injury. Thus of the twelve cattle required as murder
compensation, ten were due the chief and only two were given
to the lineage of the victim. Any delay in payment of such
compensation resulted in the chief's seizure of the requisite
wealth and usually confiscation of the total wealth of the tardy
lineage. No distinction was made between deliberate and
accidental homicide, the penalties being the same in either
case.

Murderers sometimes fled but if they did so they laid themselves open to death at the hands of the chief and the exaction
of the fine from the remaining members of their lineage. A
murderer sometimes avoided the fine and injury to his lineage
by going directly from the act to the chief, confessing, and
requesting that the chief take him as *mtung'wa* (slave). Such a
man became bound to the chief but his lot was not too difficult
and he might marry and have children who were treated much

as if they belonged to the lineage of the chief. Presumably such men ran the risk of being sold in the slave trade, however.

Although the generalization has been made that disputes within a lineage are the business of the lineage and that a chief would not normally interfere unless invited, this is not true of homicide. Killing is the prerogative of the chief as a sanction against challenges to his authority. It is never legitimate otherwise with the exception of rights a father possesses with respect to his infant offspring already noted. The chief's position with regard to homicide appears clearly in a case described to me by an elderly councillor.

Two brothers quarrelled over the possession of a cow which both claimed. One brother having failed to gain possession of the cow from the other resolved to steal it during the night and spirit it away to a cattle-client of his. He was caught in the act of leading it out of the brother's house by the owner who had been awakened by the noise. The aroused victim killed the thief on the spot but then lost his nerve and fled to another village where he had a blood brother.

The whole incident was immediately apparent to his lineage mates when they discovered the dead man the next morning. The chief (*Zumbe mkuu*) of the region heard of the incident before the day was over and his councillors had caught the murderer by the next morning. Ten cattle were demanded by the chief as payment for the death, and the murderer became a slave to the chief.

The councillor observed that the murderer should have captured his brother and delivered him to the chief who would have fined him for attempted thievery or alternatively it could have been settled within the lineage. In no case should the killing have taken place.

Brawling and drunken fighting which resulted in serious injuries also brought action from the chief within whose area the affair occurred. Small scuffles and fights which did not result in injuries were frequently settled by the lineages of the combatants but bad injuries led to ill-feeling and the possibility of retaliation. Such breaches of the peace were a direct challenge to a chief's power and could not be allowed to go further. A fine of a bull and a goat were exacted in such cases. The bull was kept by the chief as compensation for infringement on his prerogatives. This bull was divided by the chief and his councillors, the chief retaining a hind quarter, the councillors sharing the remainder. The goat was awarded to the injured party and was called 'goat of the soup'. It was said to be for 'soup to heal the injuries' (a striking parallel to such terms in American law as 'heart balm').

Theft, elopement in which the lineage of the abductor refused to pay bride-wealth, adultery, rape, and sorcery all might involve the chief.[1] Theft was almost always an interlineage or intervillage affair. It is extremely difficult to steal within a small village in which the members are in face to face daily contact and thus most stealing was of stock or food from some other village. A solitary offence was often settled by restitution between the lineages concerned. However a stock theft or other offence of similar size was a more serious matter which was usually referred to the chief of the region. The chief could exact repayment plus a fine of three goats. The fine was retained by the chief and his councillors.

Habitual thieves were a matter of serious concern to their lineages and were sometimes given in slavery to the chief. The fines of women were paid by their husbands except in cases of habitual offenders who were known to have stolen before marriage. In these cases, the women's own lineages were held liable for the fine.

Elopement is by its very nature an interlineage affair. In most cases it is a means by which a desperate young man either forces his father to produce bride-wealth for him or forces a marriage after negotiations have broken down between the father of his prospective bride and his own father. In addition, it is an act of bravado which demonstrates a young man's independence. Elopement is expensive business, however, for it requires the payment of three to four goats as fines in addition to the regular bride-wealth. Even then, after payment of the fines, the girl's father may refuse to allow marriage and demand the return of his daughter. In such a case the girl's marriage value would be damaged, however, and status as a second wife would be her best hope. Thus in most cases, elopement leads to consent to marriage by the father of the girl. However, I witnessed one case in which the father was so enraged that he refused permission for the marriage in a turbulent scene with

[1] I here use sorcery to mean magic done with intent to harm members of one's own society.

the abductor's go-betweens. His own sons were shocked and upset and tried to prevail upon him to change his mind since it meant a loss in cattle for their own prospective marriages; however, the father was adamant. A fight between the lineages nearly developed when the father of the abductor refused to pay the fine unless the marriage was allowed. At this point, the girl's grandfather summoned the local chief who managed to get the case referred to the Native Court. No decision had been rendered when I left the field but the two lineages had resumed marriage negotiations. The chief was reluctant to act except in respect to the exaction of the fine of three goats since the matter is regarded as properly a lineage affair. It appeared that he deliberately delayed hearing the case in the hope that the two lineages would amicably settle the matter eventually.

Adultery is quite frequent and is usually settled among the parties involved. Charges of adultery can only be brought by a husband against a wife; women cannot charge their husbands. Adultery is usually not grounds for divorce, although repeated offences are considered sufficient grounds. A couple caught *in flagrente delicto* can usually expect beatings from the injured husband but he must call witnesses before he can expect to get away with such a beating and also exact fines later. It is in respect to the beatings that often occur that a chief usually becomes involved, for the affair is regarded as a lineage matter otherwise. The chief is primarily concerned that retaliatory beatings are not allowed to occur and that there is no chance for a feud to develop. In cases where no violence accompanies the charge of adultery, a chief will normally not hear the evidence. In the present Native Courts, however, adultery is a recognized offence and chiefs now hear all such cases which are referred to them, although many such cases are settled out of court in traditional procedures.

Aside from homicide, sorcery is probably the most serious charge which can be brought against the individual. Like homicide, settlement of such charges is the province of the chief. An individual caught red-handed in the act of working magic against another could be stoned or beaten to death by a mob. However, such an event may be presumed to be rare since the sorcerer takes pains to conceal the actual manipulations. Accusations of sorcery are very frequent, however, particularly accusations between co-wives. Such accusations are expected and most men quite straightforwardly put them down to jealousy. If there is enough circumstantial evidence to raise suspicion, the case may be referred to the chief who then seeks confirmation from a diviner. With proper accusations and confirmation, a sorcerer could, in former times, expect death by clubbing or by being cast off an escarpment. His property was seized by the chief and his house was burnt as well. In many cases, sorcery is handled privately through counter-magic, and only when this fails is the chief called in. Nevertheless this is an area of chiefly responsibility not only through the settlement of delicts but also through action to keep sorcery under constant control. The chief is expected periodically to perform rituals to destroy the power of sorcerers. If a chief does not have the knowledge, he must hire a powerful magician to do the proper things. This is part of the obligation of chiefship, and the wealth to defray such expenses comes out of the chief's own resources.

In the Mlalo subchiefdom a very large cleansing to counteract sorcery was arranged by the chief about ten years ago. Although I did not witness it, I collected numerous accounts which agreed reasonably well with each other. This cleansing was conducted by a powerful magician of considerable fame in Tanganyika. This man was not a Shambala but was invited to the Usambara Mountains expressly for the purpose of counteracting sorcery. He was paid a fee by the chief and administered a liquid potion to everyone including children which would cause magic to act on its perpetrator and not on the intended victim. Many informants were of the opinion that it was about time to invite him back because sorcery was again occurring.

Witches are also a matter of concern to a chief. In Shambala conceptions, witch power is beyond the control of the individual. The evil power of the witch is due to a substance which may be inherited and which can harm others without the volition of the witch. Often the witch does not even know that he or she is a witch and can do nothing about the condition. It may express itself through harming someone whom the witch dislikes, by causing the witch to 'run in the night like a leopard', or by harming babies and children. A person found outside at night without clothing is almost certain to be regarded as a witch and killed on the spot by anyone. The chief sanctions such killings and acts to prevent any attempt at retaliation on the part of the lineage of the dead witch. The chief also is expected to take measures to keep witch power from being manifested, to discover witches and to help them overcome their disability. A witch who fails to submit to prophylaxis or who denies the charge even after divination has revealed the fact might be forced to submit or be killed by the chief. The death penalty for such offences is, of course, no longer enacted although Tanganyika has a Witchcraft Ordinance under which the purported exercise of occult power is an offence.

It is difficult to state principles with respect to the settlement of delicts. However there appears to be a tendency for the chief to be drawn into disputes. A distinction may be made in the types of settlements which have been discussed, however. There are first, delicts in which settlement is by compensation such as adultery or other cases involving primarily, rights over property. Secondly, there are delicts in which settlement by compensation is unlikely or impossible and fining, slavery, or execution are alternatives. The blood feud remains as an illegitimate alternative to these two. Homicide, sorcery, and witchcraft are offences for which compensation alone is not acceptable and in which the chief must act once they are brought to his attention. Other offences draw his action in so far as compensation fails to settle them and there is threat of recourse to violent self-help.

In addition to his role in the settlement of serious disputes, the control of violence and feuding, the chief performs various acts to 'keep the country'. These are primarily ritual and ceremonial actions which are intended to ward off locusts, diseases, and the raids of other tribes. The removal of the threat of raiding by the colonial government has removed an important portion of a chief's duties and value to his people, for one of the chief's major concerns in the past was the ritual and actual guarding of his people. Most chiefs are thought to possess the power of foreknowledge of raids and wars. Usually such knowledge comes in the form of a dream which must be interpreted by a diviner but it is also thought that the large sacred drum which is part of the ancestor relics of a chiefship will rumble as a warning to the chief. This drum is intimately associated with the chief. Its head is slit at his death, and a new head is fitted at the accession of the new chief. The drum must be closely watched and is only used as a signal for a serious matter such as a raid. The drum and the dreams of the chief are still considered as important sources of information about calamities. For instance, it is claimed that one of the more important chiefs had a premonition about the death of King George VI.

The chief not only provides warning of impending trouble but also takes direct action to ward off trouble. This action is both of a ritual and practical nature. Certain rituals were formerly performed along paths to make them impassable to enemies and in addition watchmen were posted by the chief. Such watchmen, called *walugoja*, were drawn from two sources. Some were men bound to the chief, generally poor men who served the chief in return for the use of his lands, the chance to gain a wife, and perhaps stock, since rich men portioned their stock out to to be kept by others. The other source of watchmen was the service due a chief by all of his subjects. In addition to duty as a watchman, such service might be labor in the fields of the chief, the clearing of paths, or service as a warrior.

Service of this kind is still due a chief although not as a watchman or warrior. At present, only the more important and powerful chiefs exact such service easily. Lesser chiefs have great difficulty in asserting their right to labor and many no longer expect it although they feel it is due them. The difficulty lies in the tax which is now paid. Chiefs are given salaries out of the taxes collected in lieu of the many kinds of service and tribute formerly claimed and little additional service can be expected. The chief has lost much through the substitution of salary for tribute and service since the salaries are low except for the highest ranks of chiefs. For this reason many heirs now refuse chiefships since a great deal of work in the enforcement of such matters as agriculture rules is expected for relatively little reward in the lower ranks either in the form of salary or prestige.

The right over services from his subjects is an important chiefly prerogative. This right also formerly extended to other rights over persons and was explicitly a right restricted to chiefs. Thus the chief could seize strangers and their goods found within his domain. Such strangers were often sold in the slave trade but also might be kept as slaves to the chief or set up under the son of a chief as a new village. A chief also took slaves of habitual trouble-makers and thieves as has already been mentioned. Poor men, orphans, and others without the security of a strong lineage, often found their way into the chief's service so that a chief's village generally was a heterogeneous collection of individuals bound to the chief by one or another tie. These rights, together with fines and the expectation of tribute, mostly in the form of a portion of the agricultural yield and a hind leg, half the breast, and the kidneys of all animals slaughtered provided the wealth out of which the chiefly establishment was supported. Much of this went out again in the form of ritual and ceremonial offerings, feasts, provisions for warriors, bride-wealth, and food for those working in the fields of the chief. However, chiefs were wealthy men and some were rapacious. Krapf records that commoners did not dare to display too much wealth for fear of inciting the lust of the paramount or the great chiefs who might seize their goods on some pretext or other.[1] However, seizure or even the exaction of tribute was not highly systematic. Krapf records the tribute collected at four villages at the mouth of the Pangani River in 1852 as being 200 yards or pieces of American calico worth about fifty or sixty dollars and he was told 'this tribute is exacted only once in every two or three years when the Vizier comes to the coast'.[2] Such practices seem to have been the standard pattern everywhere in Shambalai.

The power of a chief may be understood as primarily a right to command the allegiance of people. Power over natural resources exists, to be sure, but it is manifest in the right to command people. Although chiefs in fact hold much land and stock, the rights of each corporate lineage with respect to land and stock are similar. A royal chief may pre-empt land held by some lineage but if the lineage has given no cause through insubordination such pre-emption is simply a display of superior force and is regarded by everyone as essentially illegitimate. This is so only with respect to occupied land, however. Until recently unopened bush might be settled by anyone and right to it was established through such settlement. I do not mean to imply by this that such settlement is not subject to the explicit

---

[1] J. L. Krapf., *Travels and Missionary Labours in East Africa* (London: Trubner and Company, 1860).
[2] *Ibid.*

recognition of the chief. Allegiance to the chief is a condition
of settlement. The chief does not allot land; he demands
allegiance which is demonstrated through the rendering of
tribute and service, the carrying out of royal commands, and
attendance at public ceremonies. Failure to render such
allegiance is an invitation to destruction of a village and seizure
of its property even if ancient rights of occupation otherwise
legitimize the existing settlement. The power which the chief
exercises with respect to land is secondary; it flows from his
power to command people. In Western eyes the power over
persons and the power over resources such as land are seen to
coincide and it has been assumed by the modern authorities
that the same conditions prevail in Shambalai, especially since
it is a fact that a chief cannot tolerate a lineage in his vicinity
which refuses to recognize his right to command. Thus today,
Government sanctions the chief's claim to all unused land, and
allotment in such bush can only be made by the chief. Most
commoners dispute this vigorously, however, and it is generally
the case that commoner lineages claim their rights to land not
on the basis of assignment by a chief but simply through traditional occupation. Further, in the cases on which I have information where right is based upon allotment by some prior
holder, this allotment was as frequently made by a commoner
lineage as by a royal chief.[1]

A chief's control is not over a stretch of land with precisely
defined borders. Rather, it is over some number of lineages
which are expanding, segmenting, bringing new land under
cultivation, dying out, migrating, abandoning exhausted land
or simply maintaining their numbers. His territory is the land
of his own lineage plus the lands of every lineage which recognizes his hegemony by rendering tribute and service to him.

This is a statement of how the Shambala view the control of
the chief and is perhaps made most clear in terms of replies
to my attempts to understand the situation. When I asked
Hassani, the great chief of Mlalo, the limits of his domain, he
replied by a listing of the lesser chiefs who served under him.
I pressed him for a clearer statement whereupon he called two

---

[1] In 18 cases, 8 claimed only traditional prior occupation as justification for
land holding, 4 claimed allotment by other commoner lineages and 6 claimed
allotment by a royal chief within the last three generations.

of his councillors and together they began to list the villages each lesser chief controlled. When I attempted to state the situation in geographical terms, they made it clear that I did not understand. It was not the case that they did not know the geography. They knew their country intimately and could give vivid and detailed directions on how to go anywhere within it. It was simply that they did not conceptualize themselves as holding a block of land; what they held was the allegiance of a number of lineages. Hassani does in fact control a block of contiguous land but this spatial arrangement follows from the segmentary relations among lineages. As the royal lineage segments and new chiefships are established, there is an accretion to the area over which the senior segment possesses control. A royal chief's authority extends as far as it is acknowledged and stops only where there is some lineage which already owes allegiance to another royal chief or refuses to acknowledge allegiance to any royal chief. This has the effect of producing a spatial arrangement of the state which corresponds to the genealogical relation among royal chiefs. However, as more chiefships are created and the country fills up, the limits of each chief's jurisdiction become sharper since it is bounded more and more closely by the jurisdiction of other chiefs. Obligations would remain fluid and shifting on the peripheries but not in the more central regions of the state.

Although most of the attributes of chiefship are duplicated at all levels of the hierarchy, there are several ways in which a chief at a higher level of segmentation may express his authority over lower chiefs. This gradation in authority finds its clearest expression in rites of ancestor worship, procedures of succession to chiefship, and the appeal of legal disputes.

The operation of royal ancestor worship has been briefly examined in the case of the royal chiefs of Mlalo where it was seen that a rite directed to immediate ancestors may be performed by the lesser chief but rites directed to more remote ancestors in the royal genealogy must be carried out by a chief at the relevant higher order of segmentation. Such ritual subordination is absolute and cannot be evaded or circumvented without heavy damage to the relation between a chief and the supernatural. Most chiefs are not anxious to create such a dangerous situation for themselves. A lesser chief cannot afford frequently and openly to act contrary to the wishes of a greater chief without running the risk of the greater chief's refusal to conduct ceremonies for him.

The case of *zumbe* Shewali of Handei is instructive in this regard. Shewali was an aggressive and warlike man who conducted frequent raids against the Teita, Kamba, and Pare to gain cattle. Although he was a lesser chief under the jurisdiction of the great chief of Mlalo, these raids were carried out without sanction from the great chief and resulted in a gradual melting away of Shewali's subjects who fled to other villages even though they were getting rich in cattle. Eventually after many warnings the great chief sent warriors to punish Shewali who then fled to the sub-chiefdom of Mlola. Daffa, the great chief, then sent a message to the *zumbe mkuu* of Mlola telling him that Shewali could not expect to be present at any *fika* for his ancestors. Shewali remained in Mlola for many years and even raided his brothers' villages in Mlalo a few times. However, in his old age he returned to Mlalo and was allowed to become *zumbe* of Handei again, or at least his son was allowed to occupy the position. His return was marked by a special ancestor ceremony and relations were apparently returned to normal. However, even to this day there is resentment among other royal lineage segments in Mlalo concerning the fact that he was forgiven and some chiefs attribute the modern difficulties to the insults Shewali gave to their ancestors and feel he should have been permanently banished.

A second way in which the lesser chief recognizes the authority of higher chiefs is through the settlement of legal disputes. A dispute is the primary concern of the chief to whom the litigants owe allegiance. If it involves parties from two different chiefdoms it is either settled through the agency of the two chiefs concerned or it is referred to the great chief under whom they both serve. The examination of case material which I collected does not allow me to state with certainty whether a right of appeal existed in the past or not. Such a right does exist now under British law and most informants are confused as to whether it existed in previous times. Cory is of the opinion that no such right was recognized.[1] However, it is clear that a royal

[1] Hans Cory, 'Sambaa Law and Custom', unpublished manuscript on file at the District Office, Lushoto.

chief might refer a dispute upward in the hierarchy if he wished. This seems to have taken place in cases in which the chief did not wish to make a decision because it involved individuals from other chiefdoms or he was afraid that he could not enforce his judgment. Other sorts of circumstances in which a higher chief might become involved included charges against some lesser chief. The following case illustrates this situation.

Sighe heard when he returned to the village that the chief had gone in the night to visit the house of his (Sighe's) wife. It was said to him that the chief had only sent him so that his wife would be alone in the village. Sighe was afraid to do anything and did not even question his wife. After many days had passed, he said that he would travel to Bumbuli to visit his blood brother there and to see his cattle that he kept there. He left saying that he would be gone many days but he walked only a little way to a village where his mother's brothers were. That night he came with his mother's brother and an old man who was in that village. When they were outside his house he called, 'let me in.' His wife said, 'Who is that who calls?' When he said, she pretended not to believe and would not open the door. Everyone in the village awoke and came out to listen while Sighe broke the door and went in with the people he had brought. When all had seen that the chief was with the wife of Sighe, they left running to go to the *zumbe mkuu* at Bumbuli to claim compensation.

A long time ago they would not have dared to do that to a chief because he would have followed and killed them, but now, in this case the chief had to pay.

This case happened when the informant was a boy (perhaps 35 or 40 years ago) but was corroborated by others. Whether a chief would have killed Sighe in earlier times, I do not know. The informant was here expressing an opinion which may have been biased because he enjoyed stories of the glory and power of ancient chiefs. He could not resist telling this particular story even though it put a chief in a bad light because it is the sort of situation which warms the heart of a Shambala gossip. There are many similar cases (not involving chiefs) and they are always related with laughter and an attempt to build suspense. The conclusion in which either the husband or the lover is caught in an embarrassing situation invariably brings guffaws from the listeners.

The genealogical and ritual subordination of the lower chief is most formally expressed in the procedures of succession. Although chiefship is the vested right of a particular royal lineage and succession is restricted to the male members of that lineage, the choice of a chief involves others outside of the lineage membership. Two distinct considerations emerge from the choice of a chief. These are, first, the relation between the local royal lineage and commoners who owe allegiance to the chiefship, and second, the relation of that chiefship to the next higher chief. Both of these figure importantly in the procedures for selection of a chief and are illuminating with respect to the distribution of power and authority.

When a chief at any level including the paramount is on his deathbed, his councillors bar all visitors and make every effort to conceal the course of his illness. It is explicitly stated that this is done in order to keep the sons from attempting to seize the chiefship. The councillors send notification to the great chief, or in the case of great chiefs, to the paramount, and consult with the dying chief as to his judgment of a successor. At his death they make a decision, either abiding by his wishes or overruling them if they do not agree. This decision is not immediately announced, however, and the senior councillor (*Mlughu* or *Mdoe*) acts temporarily in the capacity of chief. When the councillors judge that they have sufficient agreement among the commoners of the chiefdom, they announce the death and declare the period of mourning. It is said that mourning lasted up to six months in earlier times. During the period of mourning, the male members of the royal lineage meet with the councillors and if they differ as to a successor there are attempts to reconcile the opposed views. In essence, it appears that whoever commands the assent of the greatest number of adherents is likely to receive the position. The councillors were in the past primarily concerned that no succession conflict should occur. However, the prominent role they played in the selection was not simply that of maintaining the peace. It was also an expression of the power which lies in the hands of the commoners. As in the myth of the creation of the state, there is an emphasis on the idea that the royal chief is a chief because the people wish him to be. A royal lineage could not usually muster enough force in its own ranks to overcome all of the commoner lineages which owe allegiance to it. Royal lineage members possess power in so far as they are able to rally commoners to their cause. They may be greatly aided in doing this by the belief in supernatural powers and by their very attitude of command, but at a succession their schisms are the power of the commoners.

It is at this point, at the naming of a candidate, that the powers of the higher chief come into play. The choice of the local lineages must be regarded in a sense as a nomination, for it must be recognized by the chief immediately above in the system. Such recognition is highly formal and begins with the dispatching of a messenger from the council concerned who conveys the name of the nominee to the higher chief. This chief in turn, recognizes the choice by sending a senior member of his council to conduct the accession. This senior councillor carries a cloth head band which he places upon the head of the nominee thus indicating recognition. At some later date, the new chief visits his superior and gives him gifts as a sign of subordination.

The installation itself is a highly important public ceremony as we have seen earlier. Most of the men owing allegiance to the chiefship in question attend, and the chief takes a solemn oath to respect the rights of his people, and to 'keep the country'. His councillors then take him on a tour of his fields and houses. Women of the chiefship, under the direction of a councillor, clear and weed the fields in an enactment of their obligations while men clean the paths and hoe any fields that require such attention. Finally, a goat is slaughtered in the midst of the banana grove belonging to the chiefship. This goat is then cooked by the chief's wives and consumed by the chief, his councillors, and the councillor sent by the superordinate chief to oversee the installation.

None of these events may take place until the dispatching of the headband which is as much a part of the legitimization of a chief as is the local ceremonial. The superordinate chief may refuse a nominee by refusal to dispatch the headband. If this is done, the procedure of nomination is repeated and must be continued until a choice suitable to the higher chief is presented. The higher chief cannot make his own nomination, however, but can only exercise a veto.

In the case of the paramount, this procedure is varied for there is no higher authority. Here a selection is made by the paramount's own council after which all the great chiefs are notified of the death and the mourning and are requested to come to Vuga. At Vuga the nomination of the successor is announced to the assembled great chiefs who must ratify it. I cannot say with certainty whether this ratification must be unanimous or whether a majority is sufficient because I could not get agreement on this issue from my informants. The succession war following the death of Kimweri *Mkubwa* and the intervention of European powers has confused the issue in the minds of the present generation of senior chiefs and councillors to the extent that they are unable to agree, but favor a simple majority. However, I am inclined to believe that unanimity was necessary from observation of the operation of other aspects of the decision making process in Shambalai. This only means the cessation of objection of course, and would clearly be an expedient course of action for a chief who found himself a minority dissentor in the selection of his own very powerful superior.

There is here a clear balance of powers such that councillors, as representatives of the local commoners, act as a powerful check upon the action of the localized royal lineage. In turn, chiefs higher in the system retain a veto which allows them to regulate, but not to dictate, the decision making process. The obligations of the new chief are made obvious to him at his installation. In most cases, local councillors expect payment for the debt of gratitude owed them by the new chief in the form of stock, beer, and numerous favors. Of course, they must give loyal service in return. The newly installed chief also feels his subordination to the chief above him. This is manifest not only in the installation itself, but also in the ritual subordination to which he is subject. The individual chief cannot deny the authority of the chiefs above him while at the same time claiming chiefship through his connection to the lineage of the higher chief. Every royal chief is in the position of balancing the requirements of his local people against the requirements of the higher chief.

A few general observations are necessary with regard to the operation of these relations of authority and subordination. The technological level of the Shambala is of the utmost importance in assessing the degree of control exercised within the chiefly hierarchy. In a society based upon simple horticulture and lacking in means of rapid communication, it may be expected that control will decrease with distance. Subsistence farming is the basis of the Shambala economy and there is little evidence of an elaborate or specialized market system in the past requiring movement of large amounts of goods and considerable control. Each chief was to a certain extent autonomous because of isolation and relative self-sufficiency. Outlying chiefs obviously would be more independent of the center than those chiefs near the capital. Thus in theory, service was due the paramount from every individual within Shambalai, but in fact it appears that labor in his fields, service as a watchman and warrior, and the like came largely from the immediate vicinity of the capital and only token service was rendered by outlying parts of the country. This is probably largely due simply to the pragmatic working out of the expenditures and returns within the system. Men who came from distant places to serve the paramount would have to be housed and fed while at the capital which might be a greater drain on the resources of the paramount than would be replaced by their service. Thus a sort of symbolic service on the part of a few courtiers sent expressly for that reason was substituted for anything on a larger scale except in case of major wars. Such conditions extended even to the raising of warriors, however. Any chief was dependent upon the agreement of lesser chiefs for the provision of warriors. It appears that the great chiefs of the outlying districts were able to check the plans of the paramount by simple refusal to raise warriors. For instance, the *zumbe mkuu* of Mlalo was in the position to refuse the demands of the paramount for warriors to intimidate the early Lutheran missionaries and the paramount had to capitulate to this stand or initiate a major war to put down this act of insubordination.[1] This was possible because of the difficulty of access and relative autonomy of the chiefdom of Mlalo which lies at a considerable distance from the capital. The same conditions applied with respect to the other border chiefdoms and must have acted as a powerful check upon the actions of the paramount. In like manner, the lesser chiefs under a *zumbe mkuu* might act as a check upon his power by

[1] I am indebted to conversations with Pastor H. Waltenberg of the Mlalo Mission for this information.

simply playing upon their isolation. Every chief must then rule as much by the astuteness of his judgment of every segment of opinion as by his command of moral and physical force.

Tendencies towards complete independence of action and breakdown in the chain of command which are inherent to some extent in a system such as this are internally countered by the relation of segments to each other. Lineage segments may be seen to lie in a hierarchical relation but they simultaneously possess coordinate relations with collateral segments of equal order. The opposition among coordinate segments is the essence of their recognition as separate entities. Since this opposition exists at every level of segmentation, it is the dynamic which creates the merging of lower orders of lineages. These lower orders merge in a greater segment defined by its opposition to other greater segments and thus create the difference in degree of power which is commanded by chiefs at the several levels.

The Council

The council is an elaborate body of advisors and functionaries which must accompany every royal chief and which is explicitly regarded by the Shambala as a balance upon the voice of the chief and upon the desires of the royal clan in general. Councillors (*wafung'wa*, pl.; *mfung'wa*, sing.) must be drawn from the commoner clans; no member of the royal clan, however distant from the chiefship he may be, can become a member of a chief's council.

The council works closely with the chief, and it is rare indeed to find a chief making a decision without the advice and consent of his council. The usual procedure in decision making is for a subject to be broached by some member of the council after which each councillor voices his opinions and there is general discussion. Finally, the chief who has remained silent announces his decision. This procedure is said to provide a chief with the wisdom of his councillors without their being influenced by his views. Once a decision has been reached upon some matter it is usual for the chief to allow his councillors to announce it in his name and to issue whatever orders are necessary. They, in turn, are then responsible for seeing that things are properly done. A proper chief seldom issues orders in public and attempts never to raise his voice, for such things are not in keeping with the dignity of his position.

Although the councillors are often referred to collectively as *wafung'wa wa kitala*, each one occupies a named position. The positions are ranked according to power and prestige and there is some differentiation of duties among them although their functions are mixed. At the present time it is difficult to understand fully the nature of each position because certain duties have dropped out and not all positions are recognized by the administration. Some councillors who formerly played important roles are now cut off from all prerogatives of office. These factors have tended to alter the council by reducing the prestige and scope of action of its members.

The composition of the council is fairly uniform throughout all chieftaincies although a few titles are localized in their distribution. The council of the paramount, however, differs considerably from the councils of all lower chiefs both in the titles of the positions and in the duties performed.

Functionaries at the capital may be divided into two categories; on the one hand, there are the ministers of state, their assistants, war captains, and messengers, and on the other hand, there are the officials of the household, the harem, and the region immediately around Vuga. In addition, there are a number of courtiers who acquire title through affinal ties to the paramount. In former times the royal establishment must have been impressive in its size. I was able to collect the titles of twenty-nine important positions from both categories and I am by no means certain that this is a complete listing. In addition to these twenty-nine functionaries there were also numerous official messengers, at least one for every great chief, and there formerly were guards and soldiers on duty to which Krapf refers, as do elderly informants.

The members of the paramount's court must all maintain residences at the capital although not all of them are necessarily drawn from the capital or its immediate environs. The paramount is expected to provide them with lands for a house and fields to support them somewhere near the capital. Most councillors maintain a residence at the capital and also residences elsewhere. They are important and powerful men and are usually polygynous with wives in the village of their own lin-

8. The residence of a minor royal chief. The living quarters and *nyumba nkuu* of a royal chief is often fenced off from the houses of other residents of the village.

9. The royal chief of Handei in the courtyard of his house of royal relics.

10. The Simbamwene of Usambara and members of his council inspecting a gift of sheep in the court-yard of the house of royal relics at the capital of Vuga. The *Simbamwene* is wearing the feather head-dress symbolic of his office.

11. The interior of a royal burial enclosure. Such enclosures are a part of each royal village and play an important role in ancestor worship and public ritual such as the installation of chiefs, war ceremonial and the like.

eage, wives at the capital, and perhaps wives located in other villages where some kin link allows settlement. Most informants agreed that in former times all of the senior councillors of the paramount were entitled to service in the form of communal field labor. All of the adults in the vicinity were expected to spend a certain number of days in each season in the fields of these men. In addition, they were given a portion of the tribute which accrued to the paramount and a part of the fines exacted in court cases. It was also customary for disputants to give them gifts before a case was heard.

The council maintains its independence of the paramount by appointing its own new members. At the occurrence of a vacancy, the remaining members gather at the house of the senior member and there nominate a man to fill the position. This nomination is then submitted to the paramount for his ratification. If the nomination is refused, the council must submit a second name, and so on until a choice suitable to both the paramount and the council is made. The paramount cannot make his own appointments, but his power of veto does regulate the choice to some extent and insures him that he will not have men on his council too hostile to him. The council may be viewed as a sort of self-perpetuating oligarchy which acts as a check upon the arbitrary exercise of power by the chief, for councillors are wealthy men. Their power stems from membership in large commoner lineages, personal possession of large herds of stock, many patron-client stock relations, blood brotherhood bonds, and affinal ties with royal lineages.

Although council positions are considered appointive and not hereditary there is a tendency for these positions to be monopolized by a few very powerful commoner lineages. Indeed, most of the senior councillors to the paramount may be drawn from only certain lineages. I am not sure about the mode of selection of the courtiers attached to the household of the paramount, but it appears that they were formerly appointed directly by the paramount. At any rate, they do not serve on the council of state or act as judges in cases, although some of them appear to have been extremely influential in that they privately swayed the opinions of the paramount.

The theory of the independence of council and chief is of extreme importance within the system, and there are a number of devices which are intended to maintain this independence. One of these, of course, is the manner of appointment of councillors. A second, no longer operative, was the *bawa njama* (*bawa*, form of the verb, to steal; *njama*, secret). The *bawa njama* was the building at the capital where cases were heard. This building was composed of two rooms, a large public room in which the councillors and interested parties convened to hear legal cases and a second room which was small and concealed and was meant for the paramount who could hear the proceedings without being seen. The usual procedure consisted of questioning of the disputants who were allowed to present their cases in turn. Anyone could put questions to either disputant although the council controlled the course of the case. After the presentation of claims and counterclaims, the councillors retired to deliberate, and at this time they might be joined by the paramount who had been listening. The paramount is said to have been able to form unbiased opinions by this method since he could hear without influencing the course of the discussion. It is likely that all of the more sophisticated Shambala were aware of the second room, but it was never known whether the paramount was present or not and only the councillors knew whether a decision had been made by the paramount or by themselves since they returned to the main room and announced the decision. There are some informants who claim that the *bawa*

TABLE II

THE PARAMOUNT'S COURT[1]

Ministers of State

Title	Duties
1. Mlughu	Chief councillor
2. Mdoembazi	Senior councillor, installs chiefs
3. Mdoe	Senior councillor, collector of tribute
4. Doekulu	Senior councillor
5. Kaoneka	Screens legal cases submitted to paramount
6. Mbaruku	War minister
7. Beleko	Assistant to war minister
8. Bilali	Assistant to war minister
9. Kiuziyo	In charge of the court calendar
10. Ngovi	In charge of magic and royal relics
11. Kibilikizi	In charge of war charms

Systems of Authority

Retainers to the Paramount

Title	Duties
1. Kihili	Head of household, harem, and lands
2. Mshakamali	Assistant to Kihili
3. Nyegere	Assistant to Kihili
4. Mashina	Head of harem guard
5. Mdimo	Major domo
6. Buga	Forerunner to paramount on journeys
7. Mgonezi	Diviner to the paramount
8. Zumbe wa chichi	Table companion to the paramount
9. Mshika funguo	Personal attendant to the paramount
10. Mlongela mpe	Usher
11. Mkikampeho	Stand-in for paramount (at his death)
12. Mlongeyampe	Messenger to region around capital
13. Mkwachasila	Messenger to region around capital
14. Zumbe wa bwene kulu	Chief of bachelors at the capital
15. Zumbe wa bwene ndodo	Assistants to above in three nearby places
16. Shemlughu	Fathers of wives of the paramount
17. Shekumlughu	Mother's brothers to the paramount
18. Mwakihiyo	Mother's brothers to Mlughu
Watawa	Representatives of nearby villages
Walau	Messengers to the great chiefs
Walugoja	Watchmen

[1] This table represents my own field observation and may be incomplete. Many offices no longer exist and informants were all unsure of their memories in giving this information. Mr. B. D. Copland collected a list in the early 1930's which is reproduced as a note in the *Journal of the East African Swahili Committee*, No. 27 (1957), p. 64, which agrees well with my list but is not as extensive. He lists two titles which I found restricted to lesser chiefs courts, and lists Kihili as executioner rather than head of the paramount's household. H. Cory provides a very incomplete list in his manuscript. *Sambaa Law and Custom* which is filed at District Headquarters, Lushoto. It agrees fairly well with my list and with Copland's but is much shorter. The titles are arranged roughly in order of seniority although I am unsure about the standing of the titles conferred by marriage.

njama was also a secret council which privately made all important decisions. It is not now possible to tell whether such a secret council existed. Many informants deny it and it is not mentioned in the writings of Krapf or Baumann but if it was truly secret this is not surprising. I am not prepared to make a judgment one way or the other about the existence of such a body

125

either in the past or at the present time. At present the term *bawa njama* is officially used to designate the council introduced by the Administration under an ordinance which altered the Native Authority of the Shambala from the chief to a chief in council. This is a completely new arrangement resulting from government reform and the ancient name was chosen to sanction the newly created body. The choice seems somewhat inappropriate.

Perhaps the most crucial importance of the paramount's council and the area in which its independence is most strongly stressed is its role in the selection of a successor to the paramountcy. The paramount cannot finally designate his heir although he may demonstrate his preference for some heir. The heir to the paramountcy is finally chosen and installed by the council of the deceased paramount. This decision is reached in conference with the great chiefs and the lineage of the paramount. The council may be viewed as playing the crucial role in the decision, for it is the *Mlughu* or chief councillor who must install the paramount, no one else having the right to conduct the rituals of installation. The council can block the desires of the great chiefs and the lineage of the paramount by refusing installation, although this is obviously a dangerous path which would not be trod without assurance of public support. Further, the *Mlughu* acts as regent during the interregnum which in former times lasted for at least six months so as to allow a proper period of mourning. It appears from what data is available that the council generally was concerned to see that the heir designated by the deceased chief actually gained the position and that the great chiefs did not force some other man more amenable to their desires into the paramountcy, or alternatively that one of the great chiefs did not himself seize the position against the wishes of the deceased. The councillors appear to have attempted to insure a peaceful succession through prompt action and the use of the *Mkikampeho* or stand-in for the chief to keep the great chiefs ignorant of the death until sufficient force could be concentrated at the capital to discourage any attempt at usurpation or succession conflict. The great chiefs were then summoned to the capital for orderly deliberations.

The independence of the council with respect to members of

the royal clan other than the chief under whom they serve is underscored by the fact that councillors are not replaced after chiefly succession but continue to serve under the new chief until they retire or die. They are relatively free of fear of losing their positions if they fail to support some one potential successor rather than some other. Councillors may only be removed through the joint action of the chief and the remaining councillors and are not easily intimidated by the threat of replacement.

In earlier times they were open to a kind of coercion by the chief however. Although they were wealthy men they were dependent on the chief for a continuing flow of income to further enhance their wealth, for tribute was given directly to the chief and then reapportioned by him among his councillors. Unlike states such as that of the Lozi, councillors were not given people and regions from which they might derive an income.[1] On the other hand, each of the senior councillors at Vuga was charged with responsibility for maintaining contact between the capital and one of the great chiefs. In this capacity, the councillor acted as host for that great chief when he visited Vuga, transmitted orders to him, received news and legal disputes from him or his messengers, and relayed tribute and information to the paramount. The senior councillors of the paramount are considered less powerful than the great chiefs, but nevertheless issue orders to them in the paramount's name. The regions for which they were responsible in the past explicitly were not their property nor were the great chiefs of the regions the subordinates of the councillors. The councillors were powerful in virtue of their private wealth, their offices, and their recognition by the paramount and the other members of the council.

Much that has been said with respect to the council of the paramount may be repeated with regard to the councils of lesser chiefs. The mechanisms through which they operate, the relations between chief and council, the powers of councillors, all of these are a repetition on a lesser scale of the paramount and his council. There are differences, however, for the councils of lower chiefs are not so clearly split into ministers and personal

[1] M. Gluckman, 'The Lozi of Barotseland in Northwestern Rhodesia', in E. Colson and M. Gluckman, eds., *Seven Tribes of British Central Africa* (London: Oxford University Press, 1951), pp. 1–93.

attendants. In the past the courts of great chiefs were large and elaborate but they did not approach the size of the paramount's establishment.

The courts of the lowest level of royal chiefs were again essentially similar to the courts of the great chiefs though still less pretentious in their operation and somewhat simpler in structure. Today all chiefly establishments are highly altered, and,

TABLE III

The Chief's Court

Title	Duties
1. Mdoe	Chief councillor
2. Kaoneka	Senior councillor
3. Mbiru	Senior councillor
4. Sheshe	In charge of legal procedures
5. Mwambashi	In charge of chief's village
6. Zizimiza	Assistant to Mwambashi, host to visitors
7. Ngovi	In charge of relics and charms
8. Mshakamali	In charge of the household
9. Kaniki	In charge of chief's fields
10. Kibirikizi	In charge of women's work and markets
11. Mtoa ngoma	In charge of war drums
12. Mtoa mshaka	Field commanders of warriors (usually two)
13. Mtoa ghunda	In charge of war horn[1]
14. Mkikampeho	Stand-in for the chief
15. Zumbe wa bwene	Chief of bachelors
16. Mpangamazi	In charge of water apportionment[2]
17. Mdoembazi	Representative of the Christians[3]
18. Watawa	Representatives of commoner villages

[1] The mtoa ghunda apparently did not exist in every royal village in which case zumbe wa bwene filled the position. All of the war leaders' positions have now dropped out.

[2] The Mpangamazi does not exist in every chiefdom but only in those areas where irrigation is practiced. This is an indigenous type of hillside irrigation in which streams are diverted above small valleys to irrigate the whole side of the valley. Canals are not used, but instead the water washes down the hillside in a sheet causing the loss of topsoils.

[3] The title, mdoembazi, was formerly meant only for an officer of the paramount's court but has been taken in modern times by an official elected by the Lutheran Mission to act as intermediary between the Mission and the Native Authority. The title has thus come to be recognized as one of the councillors of a great chief.

as in the case of the council of the paramount, certain things exist only in the memories of old informants who knew them as youths. Thus all senior councillors were formerly entitled to lands and a house in the village of the chief as well as rights to collective labor in their fields. Today only the Mdoe can expect these things.

The Mdoe occupies a position with respect to a lesser chief similar to that the Mlughu occupies with respect to the paramount. It is the Mdoe who acts during the interregnum between the death of an old chief and the accession of the new chief. The Mdoe also plays a part in the ancestor rituals of the chief and instructs a new chief in the ritual duties of his office. In former times the Mdoe travelled about the chiefdom and 'kept the land and the people'. During such travels he was preceded by musicians and wore bells on his right leg 'to tell the people of his coming'. Next to the chief, the Mdoe is the most important man in a chiefdom and is at the same time much more approachable than the chief himself. When a man has some problem or difficulty, he does not take it to the chief but takes it to one of the councillors. If it is an important problem or if he is an important man he will go directly to the Mdoe, otherwise he will go to a less senior councillor. The senior councillors of a chief carry out many duties in the name of the chief and it is only more serious or difficult matters which are brought to the attention of the chief himself. Of course, this is more often the case with respect to great chiefs than with lesser chiefs.

It is the custom for councillors to be sent by a chief to investigate the validity of claims in a legal dispute. In such cases the councillors collect gifts from the disputants and sometimes settle the case on the spot. They are also given gifts by any person who comes to them for advice, consultation, or a request to see the chief. Councillors are frequently called upon to witness the apportionment of land, and they also allot land in the name of the chief in the bush claimed by a chief. At present, chiefs claim all unopened bushland within their domains, and it is only such unoccupied lands that councillors may allot.

The councils of chiefs fill their own vacancies in a manner similar to that of the paramount's council. In most cases positions on these lower councils are more nearly appointive and are not as often held traditionally within particular lineages. This matter is highly variable, however, for in many chiefdoms the position of Mdoe is held traditionally within one commoner lineage and other positions may be. Frequently a vacancy is filled by promotion within the council and a new man is selected to fill the most junior position on the council. In many modern councils, the most junior position is that of *Zumbe wa bwene*, or chief of the bachelors. This man is in charge of the communal work and other activities of the young bachelors and the newly married men. The *Zumbe wa bwene* is usually a young man himself and is selected for his qualities of leadership displayed in the activities of boys such as herding and dancing. For an ambitious man the position of *Zumbe wa bwene* is often the first step on the ladder of political success. Success might culminate in the position of senior councillor to a great chief or even service in the court of the paramount, for councillors are not always chosen from the local region. It appears that famous councillors from lower courts were sometimes called to the capital to serve under the paramount. Some of these men were even sent out as regents if there were no royal son or brother available. The councillors cannot be viewed as transferrable civil servants, however, for it was not the usual thing for a man to move up from chiefdom to chiefdom.

The greatest utility of the councillor lays in his intimate knowledge of affairs in his chiefdom. It is this knowledge upon which he relies in settling disputes, in calling for communal work and the like. It is true that there are standard fines for certain types of offences but these are not uniformly applied. Judgments are made at least partly upon ability to pay. A wealthy lineage is liable to be assessed a larger fine in a dispute than is a poor lineage, a rich man is likely to be treated differently than a poor man. The chief knows a great deal about his chiefdom, but some of the great chiefs have held regions which must have had populations of twenty-five to thirty thousand as Mlalo has today. In a chiefdom as large as this a chief must rely heavily upon his councillors for intimate knowledge of people and places. Even the council as a whole cannot know all of the details which might be useful but the chances are greater if all of the councillors are local men. Further, the close personal relations between the chief and his councillors and the multitudinous ties which bind them together do not make transfer too likely. Although the chief and the council represent two sources of power in the system, they normally operate together in close and mutually supportive harmony. Together they are, in the Shambala view, a remarkably satisfactory government.

Chapter VII

ECONOMIC ASPECTS OF
THE POLITICAL SYSTEM

I T is most difficult at this time to reconstruct the flow of goods and services which supported the administrative structure of the state in earlier times. Furthermore, it is equally difficult to speak with confidence of the nature and extent of public enterprises within the system. It is nevertheless profitable to attempt this task because to do so fills out the picture of the power and responsibilities of chiefs and of councils. Today, of course, it is primarily personal taxes and cesses upon agricultural commodities which provide the income of the officials and employees and the operating costs of the government services in which these employees and officials participate. The economics of the present local government have been over 70 years in the making and there are now very few men who can remember what it was like before taxes set at official rates by Europeans were instituted. The older flow of wealth has disappeared in nearly all respects, for the European administration has not thought it practical nor useful to retain it, even though the hierarchy of chiefs and councillors it supported has been retained. Indeed, as elsewhere in Africa, strong attempts were made from the beginning to introduce a money economy, eliminate tribute payment in goods, and place the chiefs and other officials on a salary basis. Thus only a few of the dynamics of this earlier economy can now be observed. I must rely on fragments of information and upon recollections, often from single informants, which cannot be cross checked by other informants or by observation of the system in operation.

The Nature of Public Enterprises

It does not now appear that the public enterprises in which the state engaged were particularly complex or numerous. There was, of course, the mounting of military operations both to annex surrounding areas and to defend the mountains against the raids of the Masai, Kwavi, and others. All adult males were obligated to serve as warriors under their local royal chiefs and in turn these chiefs were obligated to provide warriors to the great chiefs who finally had the obligation to provide warriors for the paramount. As far as I can tell from the writings of early Europeans, there was no standing army which had to be paid for constantly. The paramount depended upon the rapid raising of warriors through an efficient network of messengers and upon a small group of *walughoja* or watchmen who were drawn in rotation from nearby villages to provide the armed force necessary for his protection and his conquests. It appears that soldiers were expected to live off the country and to gain their pay from shares in the booty of war, or when collecting tribute, from a portion of the proceeds. Mwankali, the retired *zumbe* of Handei who fought in the last wars before the Germans came and who later served in German expeditions in the mountains and in the 1914–18 war explained it in the following fashion:

> In the old time when there was war, the horn called *ghunda* was used to call the men out but the drum was used too so men knew it from the call to work. The man who blows the horn was called *mtoa ghunda*, and *mtoa ngoma* made the drumming. He stayed in the village but *mtoa ghunda* and the *watoza mashaka* led the men to fight. The young men came behind with *mdoe* to help and to learn from men who had fought before.
>
> Everyone had a spear and a shield and a big knife and some had guns but *watoza* were big men and didn't carry shields. When we won we took the women and children and married them and sold the men to the Arabs, and *zumbe* divided the cattle and goats and sheep to the *watoza*. *Zumbe* would send his brother or his son to that new village along with brave warriors who took the fields there. Men who ran away or hid when *gunda* called, they didn't get anything and had to make many bundles of sharp stakes to put in the ground around a village as a barrier from enemies.

Krapf notes that disobedient soldiers were sold into slavery and modern informants corroborate this punishment.[1]

[1] J. L. Krapf, *Travels and Missionary Labours in East Africa* (London: Trubner and Co., 1860), p. 385.

It was apparently not unknown for the Shambala to hire mercenaries from other tribes for the purpose of conducting wars. This was done during the civil war between Semboja and Kiniassi when Semboja employed coastal troops to fight the Zigua along the Pangani River.[1] He was probably forced into this by the unsettled nature of the country and his inability to raise sufficient warriors by any other means. Baumann does not say how Semboja proposed to pay these mercenaries but he presumably promised them the spoils of the battle for Baumann reports that this was the arrangement in other agreements with the Masai and the Chagga.[2] Informants described a similar arrangement which Semboja made with the Teita to drive Kiniassi and Shekulavu out of Vuga:

> Semboja sent a safari with three Wakilindi to lead it, one of them named Sejengo. They went to Teita and brought many men to fight. They covered the country like locusts, they took all—cows, goats, sheep, and people. This is called *nkondo ya mazola* (war of taking everything). Many villages were burned, even Vuga. Many people hid in the forest or in caves. When the fighting came to Vuga no one would fight because all the men had gone to Gare and Mamba to ambush the Teita. When they saw the fires, they came back and drove the Teita away. There was much fighting and Shekulavu was killed at Kwatango. That fighting ruined Shambalai because many were killed and others the Teita sold as slaves. Finally Semboja made those Teita go but the fighting didn't stop and Semboja and Kiniassi and his uncle Chanyeghela all sold people to the Arabs. It was a bad time and many men got the habit of just taking goats and chickens and whatever they wanted because that is the payment of warriors.

Certain other enterprises besides warfare were considered to be in the public interest and were accomplished under the orders of royal chiefs. These included the construction and repair of houses for chiefs and senior councillors, the maintenance and construction of palisades around villages and royal harems, the maintenance of royal burial places, the construction and maintenance of roads and paths including the planting of hedges along such paths to keep stock out of fields, and irrigation canal construction and repair. Such projects were decided upon by

---

[1] Oscar Baumann, *Usambara und Seine Nachbargebiete* (Berlin: Dietrich Reimer, 1891), pp. 192-3.

[2] Baumann, *ibid.*, p. 193.

the chief and his council and were announced to the people by
zumbe ya bwene (chief of the bachelors) who supervised the work.

Zumbe ya bwene called out the news of *ghunda* work in the evening
when people were eating and would hear him. He would visit
with them and tell them of the work to be done. Early the next
morning he would play the *ghunda* and shout out for people to
assemble and then the work would start. A man who had the
skill would walk around and play the *zumai* (a flute with a reed)
for the work. If they were building a house, people would be told
long before and the poles and thatch would be cut and brought
to the proper place and everything would be ready for the work.
After the work was finished, *zumbe* would feed the people with
meat and sugar cane beer. Any food that was left, the women
they would take it home to eat in the morning.

Such obligatory communal labor is still practiced on various
community projects including school and roads but it is given
grudgingly because of tax payments; there is no feasting afterwards, and chiefs attempt to keep it to a minimum. Indeed,
lesser chiefs seldom are able to command it today and only
great chiefs and the paramount receive such service regularly.
No councillors at any level are regarded as having the right to
command such labor and younger men deny that they ever did,
although old men say they did.

Chiefly establishments and the royal court were also public
costs to some extent. The great council hall, the *Bawa njama*,
and the house called *Burira* where royal relics were kept were
built with public labor and the messengers and courtiers to the
paramount were maintained out of the tax and tribute that
came into the paramount. In the same sense, the fines and fees
levied by courts went to maintain the councillors and chiefs
who held those courts. Very little in the way of indemnities or
damages was paid to injured parties but instead fines were used
to pay the costs of the courts themselves. There is a clear notion
among the Shambala that the dispensing of justice is a public
business and that private self-help is an illegitimate activity.
This is not to say that there was an accounting system for courts
and a central treasury for the collection of fines and the like.
As far as could be determined by my investigations all courts
operated independently with the revenues going to the local
chiefs and councillors. Any appeal that might be made upward

through the courts required new payments to higher courts. I cannot be certain from the information available to me whether a reversal of a decision was accompanied by a refund of any fines or seizures made by a lower court. It would seem logical to assume that such was the case or appeals to a higher court would be meaningless. However, it may be that there was no right of appeal but only the possibility of referral upward by the court itself. There are cases, however, in which litigants unsatisfied with the conduct of a case before the court of a lesser chief have been successful in getting a great chief to intervene for them.

Sources of Income

The income to support public enterprises and the administrative hierarchy was derived from many sources. We have mentioned service in the form of labor and warriorship and fines and court fees also include the collection of taxes and tribute, the right of seizure of the property and persons of aliens and strangers within Shambala territory, the monopoly on the slave and ivory trades, ritual and ceremonial rights as in the formal apportionment of meat from animals slaughtered, and income from chiefly lands.

Other sources were: caravan fees, war booty, and personal gifts for political patronage. Beyond these perquisites of chiefship, there are of course, the service obligations of a cattle herder to his patron which would yield considerable to a wealthy chief but which are not the exclusive rights of chiefs, and the flow of wealth from marriages which has the same status.

By far the most regular of the sources of income appear to have been tribute, service, fines and fees, produce from chiefly fields and gifts for patronage. The seizure of strangers must have been a relatively rare event, as would also be true of war booty, but not caravan fees. As has been previously mentioned the course of the Pangani River was an important caravan route and this route passed for many miles through Shambalai. It is quite clear from Baumann's writings that a caravan toll was charged by the Shambala at the time he was there but it is unfortunately not clear what this toll amounted to. Baumann records that Semboja installed his sons Muassi and Buiko along the Pangani River to collect from the caravans.[1] This toll was not only expected from the Arab caravans but was also collected from the Zigua and Pare. Shambala control of this route was always contested, however, and sometimes broken. Thus the Zigua defeated Kimweri Mkubwa's armies and broke his hold on the area because they were the first to acquire guns. Semboja later reinstated Shambala claims in the area but again lost them to the Zigua in 1889 because of the weakening of the state through internal war over succession. Before that event, however, Semboja had taken all the goods (amounting to 250 head loads worth about DM. 15,000) belonging to the expedition under Dr. Hans Meyer. This was regarded as an outright theft by Meyer and Baumann of course, but it is explained by the Shambala as being within the seizure rights of the *Simbamwene* when unexplained strangers enter his territory. It is extremely difficult to assess the revenue from such tolls and seizures but it could have been considerable. However, Gray is of the opinion that the Pangani–Usambara–Kilimanjaro route was not heavily used by the Arabs and cites good evidence to support this position.[2] This does not mean that there was not considerable non-Arab traffic on this route, however, for ivory came this way to Pangani according to Krapf.

In addition to whatever could be gained by such tolls, the *Simbamwene* also profited from trade himself. Baumann states that many captives taken in the war over the paramountcy between Semboja and Kiniassi were sold on the coast as slaves in the very extensive slave trade. This means of dealing with insurgents and common criminals is still widely known among Shambala informants who told me it was in use until well into the time of German administration. In this way the paramount could not only get rid of trouble-makers but could do it at a profit as well.

Taxes and Tribute

The exaction of taxes and tribute was a major right of the *Simbamwene* and provided much of the revenue which supported

[1] Oscar Baumann, *op. cit.*, p. 190 *passim*.
[2] Sir John Gray, 'Trading Expeditions from the Coast to Lakes Tanganyika and Victoria Before 1857', *Tanganyika Notes and Records*, No. 49 (1957), p. 242.

the whole chiefly hierarchy. One of the principal functions of the *walau*, or messengers of the paramount, was the transmittal of tax orders from the capital to the great chiefs. These *walau* appear to have been not only messengers but also assessors and represent a strengthening of the executive arm outside of the chiefs themselves. Indeed they represent an important check on the power of the great chiefs as against the *Simbamwene*, for they seem to have had the power to deliver a tax quota to the great chief and then to audit it upon delivery to Vuga. An old retired chief explained it in the following way:

> The *zumbe mkuu*, he had a requirement from Vuga. *Mlau* told him how much cattle and sheep and goats and thatch grass and poles and other things he must give. But *mlau* didn't get it. *Zumbe* went to the people (literally to the lineage heads and the council) and they gave him things for the good year, and the rain, and the *fika* he had done to keep the people. *Zumbe* took those things and went to Vuga himself. He stayed with *mlau* and then he would go to *Simbamwene* and say, 'look, these things I have brought you.' *Simbamwene* would kill a black bull from those and he would keep a leg with the tail and other parts and those old men who sat with him and *zumbe* would eat the rest.

Apparently the great and lesser chiefs could overfill their quotas and thus retain a portion for their own use while delivering the demanded quota to the higher authorities. This seems the meaning of the following:

> We people, we gave gifts to *zumbe*. He didn't have to ask us. We gave for his rain and because it isn't good for common people to have much and *zumbe* little. The *Simbamwene* would see it and take it, while he only takes part of what *zumbe* has. We used to have a proverb; 'you cannot find your pot? then look at the *kitala*.' It has two meanings you see. It means everything finds its way to the *kitala* but it also means *zumbe* keeps the people and helps them when there is nothing.

The system worked somewhat differently on the coast where the subjects were not Shambala but 'Swahili' and Digo. Here high councillors were dispatched directly from Vuga and collected personally rather than relying on the local chiefs and *walau*. This could probably be properly called tribute while the system used in the mountains is closer to tax. Krapf witnessed collec-

12. Early arrivals at a market. Markets are held weekly in designated villages under the regulation of the local chief who maintains order and keeps the market place clear. Women selling produce cluster in the center while the men dealing in other commodities form an outer ring. Only the snuff sellers erect their umbrellas.

13. The market at its height is a closely packed melee of women clad in bright *kangas*. The lorries of a buyer from town can be seen in the background.

15. Kimweri Mputa Magogo, Q.M., the Simbamwene of Usambara, wearing the sacred hat of office and a robe handed down from his father's reign.

14. *Zumbe mkuu* Daffa, the former great chief of Lushoto who was retired at the time this picture was taken. Daffa wears a robe presented to him by

tion at Pangani on the coast in 1852 and describes it in the
following fashion:

At break of day the war horn sounded, and a soldier ran up and
down the village shouting with a loud voice, 'Get ready, ye
Wasambara soldiers, the Mazumbe, the kings (the vizier and two
governors), are about to depart.' The whole village was at once in
motion; for the people were glad of their departure, the soldiers
having behaved to them with violence, and robbed them of
poultry and other things, and the owner of the house in which I
was had buried his valuables out of fear of the soldiery. The
tribute paid on this occasion by the Pangani people to king
Kimeri was not very large, consisting of 200 yards of Americano,
Lowel calico, of the value of from fifty to sixty dollars. This tribute
is exacted only once in every two or three years, when the vizier
comes to the coast.[1]

This tribute was paid by four villages which Krapf estimated
contained 4000 people, and further tribute was collected at
another village about three leagues away. Although this collection might not have been yearly along the coast it was being
collected from people who also owed some loyalty to the Sultan
of Zanzibar. In the mountains proper, it was more regular and
was not accomplished by soldiers but by local chiefs.

In the case of this tribute, Krapf witnessed Kimweri's receival
of it and his subsequent distribution which elderly councillors
tell me was proper with all taxes and tributes.

... he had received the tribute brought by the vizier from the
coast, consisting of 200 pieces of Americano, and a number of
oxen and sheep. Of the 200 pieces of cloth the king retained 100 for
himself and his wives, giving forty-two to the vizier (*Mdoe*) and
his soldiers, thirty three to the headman of Fuga, and twenty-five
to Mbereko and his servants.[2]

Councillors at Vuga today when asked about this particular
division expressed the opinion that the forty-two went to *mdoe*
to give to *mlughu* who is really chief councillor to the *Simbamwene*
and who even today is served most directly by *mdoe*. The headman of Fuga (*sic.*) they thought must be the rest of the council,
while *mbereko* would distribute the twenty-five to the soldiers
over whom he was commander. They questioned Krapf's
failure to say how the oxen and sheep were apportioned or how

---

[1] J. L. Krapf, *op. cit.*, p. 375.   [2] *Ibid*, p. 396.

many there were since these were normal tax except along the coast.

In the same place Krapf describes the sentence passed on a man who refused to pay tax, killed three soldiers, and fled. His 'relatives' were seized, and by this I assume his lineage-mates are meant, he was ordered to be captured and brought to Vuga for execution, and his children were ordered to be sold as slaves.[1] This passage is interesting for also containing reference to a 'state prison' at Vuga. This may have been a quarters where slaves were collected before being sent to the coast in batches since prisons are relatively rare in states of this nature because prisoners are an expense only a rich country can afford.

In most cases it appears that stock was the proper medium of tax payment but other things were also used. Thatch grass and house poles are frequently mentioned and maize was also given:

> My grandfather kept a field near the *kitala* for *zumbe*. It was my grandfather's field but he always grew a crop on it to give to *zumbe*, and not to eat himself. Many *wazumbe wadodo* didn't do this but my grandfather always did. He always gave maize or maybe sugar cane beer or honey. We don't give those gifts anymore but *mdoe* gets taxes from us every year. It's not like a gift now and people don't give it out of pride but because they must. Before we gave what we had so that a smith would give hoes or knives and old men gave cattle which they and their sons took to the *kitala* where everyone would see and *zumbe* would kill a goat and they would cook it and eat it there.

Although there was certainly an obligation to pay, it was phrased as gifts and small returns were given by the chief. Taxes payed to the chief were termed *ndugush* or gifts, this word having the connotation of an obligation. The small return given by the *zumbe* was termed *ntulo* which also means gift but does not carry the connotation of obligation, that is, gifts freely given out of esteem.

Ndugush was also sent by a newly installed *zumbe* to the chief above him who had approved his installation. The present *zumbe* of Shashui describes it thus:

> When a *zumbe mkuu* sends his son to the people as a *zumbe mdodo*, the son should send him stock in a year or maybe two. This will be

[1] J. L. Krapf, *op. cit.*, pp. 396–397.

called *ndugush.* The *zumbe mkuu* does this too. He goes to *Simbamwene* with maybe twenty men and the cattle and *Simbamwene* kills a black bull for them and they kill a billy goat for him and they all will eat with those old men at the *kitala,* the *wafung'wa* and the *walau.* To take cattle to the *kitala* is *mzugilo* and the cattle are *ndugush.* The black bull, that is *ntulo* of the *Simbamwene.*

The payment of taxes did not terminate the obligation to chiefs. There was, in addition, the requirement of service. The service as a warrior has already been discussed with its rewards and its punishments, as has the labor due the chief on what were deemed public projects. Such service was also due from both men and women on a regular basis and was under the direct control of the chief and council. All royal chiefs were due this type of service. Ali, the *mdoe* of Mlalo, explained it in these words:

> Every day two men and two women came to work at the kitala. *Zumbe ya bwene* would tell them the night before that they must come and if they could not he would remember and call them again. A man who did not come must pay a chicken, if he did not come the next day, another chicken. Women paid clay pots sometimes, sometimes chickens. These people worked in *zumbe's* fields, Nowadays old men who don't pay tax work in *zumbe's* fields every Saturday.

Not only was such labor forthcoming for very large public projects as determined by the chief and council, but as this informant makes clear it was due in regular rotation simply to maintain the royal households. This type of labor was also carried out for *mdoe,* but not for the other members of a chief's council. It was due all the councillors at the capital of Vuga, but not the *walau.*

Fines and Fees

A wide variety of fines for offences were imposed. I have specified some of these in previous chapters and there made it clear that delicts had a tendency to become public and to require compensation, not just to the injured party but to the chief and council to re-establish equilibrium. Thus blood compensation requiring the payment of twelve cattle was apportioned ten to the chief and council, two to the injured lineage. Of these cattle, the chief appears to have kept nine, the council slaughtering and dividing the tenth. Assault cases with serious injury also incurred a fine of one bull which was slaughtered and divided, the chief receiving a hind quarter and the council, the remainder. Theft was punished by a fine of three goats of which two usually went to the chief and one to the council. Property seizure by the chief was common in sorcery, witchcraft, and murder where the offender refused to pay the fines. Usually it involved seizure of the property of the whole lineage, but negotiations later could lead to a partial return of goods belonging to those other than the offender. Such property appears to have been apportioned about half to the chief and half to the council and warriors who carried out the punishment. The offender, his wives and children were taken as slaves and sold or kept by the chief. Sorcerers were killed on the order of the chief. Insubordination to any chiefly order by a commoner lineage also called for fines.

Shewali commanded his people to gather to fight his enemies but the people of one village did not come and told *mdoe* they would not fight in Shewali's wars any more. Shewali sent soldiers and they took all the cattle and small stock of the village. After that the village was afraid and the people went to *zumbe* Daffa and he gave them land. I forgot what that village was called. It is gone and the people went to Kitivo to live with Shewali's brother. Shewali fought so much most of his people left and he had many cattle but no people. It was a long time before this village grew large again. But when Shewali was young it was big, almost like Mlalo where the *zumbe mkuu* stays. Even Shewali left for a while and took his *chengo* to Mlola but I came back here to be *zumbe* when my father was old and all of our *chengo* came then and even my father Shewali came and died there. It is his *kitala*.

Any court case which was brought to a royal chief came first to a councillor. If the disputants were important men, they would seek out *mdoe* or *mlughu* but most cases came to *sheshe* or, on the paramount's council, to *kaoneka* since these men were responsible for screening cases and might settle simple disputes and had often acted as witnesses to the earlier events which gave rise to the dispute. Gifts were given by the disputants and were viewed as simple fees. The carryover of this pattern often leads to charges of bribery today, but it was not viewed as extortion or bribery in earlier times. Such fees did not usually go to the chief but were a right of councillors. It is not unknown, however, for chiefs to receive them. They were seldom more than a goat or a few pots of beer.

Various fees were collected by the chief and council in respect to land law. I have previously made clear that the chiefs were not viewed as owning all land but they entered land transactions in a number of ways. No chief could allow strangers to settle near him who were hostile, and thus migrants had to have permission to settle an area. However, several categories of land were available. There was first *tundui* which is unopened bush land. All informants, royal and commoner, to whom I talked claimed that *tundui* could be opened by any man and although it was proper to notify the *zumbe* of intention and even request councillors to witness the clearing for a small fee, the chief did not allot such land. Today *tundui* is controlled by chiefs with Government sanction.

Land previously cultivated or claimed by royal lineages by virtue of first occupancy, seizure, or inheritance or because it is not now legitimately held by some commoner lineage is termed *ngao*. It cannot be settled without chiefly allotment. This task is usually delegated to councillors who receive a fee of a goat for allotment and for witnessing the boundaries. At the death of the holder, his heirs are liable for a kind of tax termed *dezu*. This is a small portion of the *ngao* which reverts to the chief and becomes *ngao* again. It may be re-allocated by the chief and was, in the past, mainly plantain plots. If an *ngao* holding is small the heirs may redeem *dezu* by paying the chief a goat instead. Today this is the usual practice. Land that has been legitimately alloted by a chief is subject to *dezu* for two generations but after that no further fees are required and the occupant has clear title. A situation rather similar to *dezu* exists for house plots in a *kitala* village. A man who is given a house plot in a royal village cannot sell the plot, and a gift or fee must be sent to the chief before his heirs may occupy the house.

In all chiefly allotments *ndugush* (a cattle gift) should be sent to the chief within a couple of years. Grazing land is commonage and is under the chief's protection. If a man should attempt to bring grazing land under cultivation, the chief must evict him, fine him a goat, and have any structures or fences removed. The same holds for areas designated as market places.

The Domestic Income of Chiefly Households

It is necessary to consider not only those sources of revenue which we may conceptualize as public such as tax, tribute, corvee labor, and the like, but also to consider the private resources of chiefs. There is no hard and clear distinction within Shambala society between the public treasury and the private wealth of chiefs. A chief is expected to meet his obligations, to dispense largess, provide hospitality, conduct ceremonies and provide sacrifices of cattle, sheep and goats. It is also recognized that he can only do this if his people provide him with the wherewithal, but no careful accounting is kept by anyone as to whether he profits or does not. Wealth that comes to the chief is his to manage. He may be a profligate and mismanage it so that in the end he is put under pressure or even unseated in favor of someone else. Thus we may say there is some ultimate check upon his behavior, but in general the tax or tribute that comes to him is used as he sees fit. Thus chiefly households are often large with many dependents working small plots of land in return for which they run errands, provide armed support, herd stock, and work the chiefs' own fields. The chiefs may judiciously employ the wealth of his lineage as well as the tax and service due him to maintain his position or even to increase his holdings and his following.

The size and wealth of chiefs' households vary a great deal, but they are nearly always larger than commoners' holdings. Krapf commented on the harem that Kimweri maintained at Vuga as looking like a village itself all enclosed and well guarded. He estimated that Kimweri possessed 100 wives and stated that each wife had her own fields. The *Simbamwene* had retainers whose duties were specifically the management of the royal lands and the direction of the wives' work. However, I have no reliable figures to indicate how extensive the holdings of Kimweri or earlier paramounts might have been. The present *Simbamwene* has fairly large holdings including about 5 acres of coffee. He also has some fallow land, but the total amount he holds is unknown.

The average size of land holding for a head of household in the more densely settled parts of Shambalai was approximately 3·5 acres in 1957 so that the paramount is comparatively very rich in land. Indeed my surveys indicated that half of the household heads in three villages held 2 acres or less.

Great chiefs appear to hold less land than the paramount but not a great deal less. I was unable to get figures on all the great chiefs, but all that I questioned indicated holdings slightly smaller than those of the paramount, while two who I was able to check directly held between 20 and 28 acres. Like the paramount, these men had some fields in coffee and some fallow land as well as a substantial area planted in bananas which was supposed to remain in this crop as a security against bad years. Lesser chiefs hold less land but considerably more than most commoners. Holdings of twelve lesser chiefs ranged between 7 and 18 acres in my 1957 survey.

In all cases the chiefs not only held substantially larger acreages than most commoners, but had the very considerable added advantage of holding most of it in large blocks. An Agriculture Department survey carried out in 1947 in the Mlalo Basin indicated that the average household head held approximately seven small fields at an average distance of 23·58 minutes walking distance from his home.[1] Thus most cultivators spend a large portion of their time simply getting to their fields and correspondingly less time in productive agricultural labor.

In the light of these factors it is clear that all chiefs can obtain more food from their land than is necessary for the average minimum needs of a Shambala household at the present time. This is not to say that the average Shambala is adequately fed. He is most assuredly not, for the diet is not well balanced and it is especially low in animal proteins. However, it is clear that chiefs are better fed than most others and that they produce surpluses above their own needs. However, the patterns of hospitality, the food for ceremonies, aid to the needy, the feeding of work parties, and a host of other such obligations must be met. All Shambala recognize this and judge a chief partly by his largess, while at the same time admitting quite freely that the chief must have adequate resources if he is to dispense this largess.

I found it extremely difficult to discover the stock holdings of any Shambala. The patterns of stock clientship result in most

---

[1] Report of the Mlalo Rehabilitation Scheme. Oct. 1949 Manuscript on file, The Agriculture Office, Lushoto, Tanganyika.

owners holding very few animals at their own homes. They are, furthermore, extremely reluctant to divulge the amount of stock they hold for several reasons. It is useful to conceal one's actual political strength but to hint that there are many cattle clients. It also lays one open to harmful stock magic to tell where stock is and by whom it is being kept. Besides these traditional reasons, there are the modern reasons of tax evasion and avoidance of agricultural scheme rules relating to the placement and care of stock. Thus few chiefs were willing to talk about their own stock holdings. In only two cases was I able to get any kind of reliable estimate of the cattle holdings of chiefs. In both cases the men were great chiefs and they were regarded as wealthy in cattle. One of these men had 65 cattle and over 100 goats and sheep, the other had slightly more than 100 head of cattle and an equal number of small stock. The veterinary officer stated that he thought the ownership of more than 30 head of cattle was quite rare and the Mlalo Basin survey indicated an average holding of 2 cattle and 2 small stock for that region. However, Mlalo is poor in stock compared to certain subchiefdoms such as Mlola, and it is furthermore doubtful that an accurate determination of stock ownership as distinct from clientship was possible in that survey.

As in the case of land, however, it seems certain that chiefs hold greater than average numbers of stock, have more opportunity for swelling their herds, and invest this wealth judiciously to increase their political following. They also must slaughter more often, however, and probably represented in earlier days the main source of meat for most people as well as the active focus in a small constant flow of stock wealth.

If adequate figures were available it would probably be possible to demonstrate a rather rapid and fairly well balanced turnover in stock with chiefs acting as the major intermediaries. Thus stock flowed into the chief as tax and tribute, as fines, and as bride-price payment for his daughters. At the same time it was paid out in ceremonies, hospitality, and in bride-price payments for the chief's own wives and for the wives of his sons. It is likely that a chief had some excess of intake over expenditure in this movement of stock, but not a great excess.

Bride-price payments are not high in Shambalai if compared with those in many pastoral societies, but they are sufficiently high to cause young men much difficulty and provide a major incentive for economic activity within the society.[1] In eleven marriages which I investigated in 1956 the average cost was 2 bulls, 1 cow, 3 goats, 4 gallons of honey and 24 shillings. This was in addition to gifts of dresses, shoes, perfume, and beads to the prospective bride during courtship which might cost the suitor as much as 100 shillings. It also does not include birth payments following marriage nor small gifts of beer, tobacco and the like paid out to the girl's father while negotiations are under way.

The stock paid out as bride price by a chief does not appear to be greater in amount than that paid by any other man, but a chief may be expected to treat the lineage of a prospective bride to somewhat more lavish gifts of other items. Some informants insisted that in ancient times chiefs paid no bride price at all, which would place a somewhat different light on the circulation of stock wealth, particularly in view of the large numbers of wives some chiefs maintained. Mwankali, *zumbe* of Handei, claimed that:

> In the old time a *zumbe* could see a girl and like her. Then he would send a cloth to her father's door and everyone else would leave her alone. She was called *mkwe mzumbe* then and later she would go to marry him. He might send the *mpombe* (bride-price cattle) but he didn't need to. He would pay *usangusawa* (1 goat to the bride's mother on proof of virginity) though, because it was his pride to do it.

Informants disagree about this right of chiefs to claim women without payment and it seems likely to have been an essentially illegitimate act which nevertheless might well be carried out by very powerful chiefs. Commoners might fear the consequences of appealing to a higher chief for adjustment of such a case. In any event, all informants denied that such a practice could extend to anyone but a reigning chief. No other royal clansman, even a chief's son and heir apparent, had such a right.

The chief's household was a kind of center of economic activity in Shambala society. The institutions of this system acted to

[1] For a stimulating discussion of the economic analysis of bride price see Robert F. Gray, 'Sonjo Bride-Price and the Question of African "Wife Purchase" ', *American Anthropologist*, Vol. 62, No. 1 (1960), pp. 34–57.

focus economic resources here. Thus the religious system centered upon rituals conducted by or for the chief and requiring the provision of animals for sacrifice and food for the consumption of the public who attended and from whom ultimately, the food and stock came. In a similar way, the legal system brought fines and fees in, the marriage institutions directed stock and other resources in and the waging of warfare yielded booty through the chief's organization of its strategy. In a host of other ways as well—cattle lending, public works, prestige competition, the institution of chiefship provided the motivation for production beyond the needs of the individual cultivator and also the machinery for the investment of that production. It seems clear that the chiefs themselves profited most from the workings of this state, but it was not completely without profit for the common citizen who received security from the slave trade and from raids, whatever pride comes from membership in a successful political entity which dominates its region, an orderly system for the redress of wrongs, supernatural benefits which I find difficult to measure but which have a cultural reality that is still discernable today, and a certain amount of status achievement mobility by which it was possible to rise to high rank as a councillor or *mlau* and wield considerable economic and political power. Although the evidence is fragmentary I believe the major outlines of the flow of authority and of the concomitant flow of wealth emerge clearly enough. The specialization of administrative functions had proceeded far enough in the Shambala state so that a structure of offices with prerogatives and responsibilities existed. This was most highly developed in the communications and financial areas where the office of *mlau* enabled the paramount to maintain a current estimate of the economic conditions in each sub-chiefdom and to gauge and meet the requirements of his own treasury thereby. There was sufficient play in the system to allow every chief to maintain his own establishment in the proper style and still meet the requirements from above. Very few of the economic prerogatives considered were the exclusive right of the paramount. Again the duplication of powers at all levels of the system emerges clearly.

The case of Shewali, the chief of Handei which was cited makes it clear that a chief could not persist in onerous and unusual demands for service and tribute without facing the prospect of losing his subjects. Shewali, through his continuous warfare, caused his people to openly resist his commands and although he was legitimately able to exact fines for this he nevertheless lost subjects to other chiefs. There were checks in the system then, where the power of the commoners was made plain to a chief. Otherwise, Shewali's people could not have fled and received succor from a higher chief, in fact, Shewali's own father. In the same way, Great Chiefs were able to resist the demands of the paramount if they became unusually heavy or unreasonable. A case in point was the refusal of the Great Chief of Mlalo to supply soldiers against the missionaries which I have cited elsewhere. The balance of chief against chief and commoners against the chiefly hierarchy apparently acted to control exorbitant demands while still providing the revenue to maintain chiefs in a fitting style.

Chapter VIII

CONCLUSIONS

WITHIN Shambala society the division of members into discrete corporate groups of kinsmen on the basis of the lineage principle must be identified as a major institutional complex. Membership in corporate patrilineages is of vast importance in the definition of territorial residence, in inheritance of rights in property, in the flow of authority, and in religious observances. Internally the lineage may be highly differentiated on the basis of kinship position and relative seniority but externally it is a unit with corporate rights and corporate responsibilities. Every such lineage possesses a leader who is essentially *primus inter pares*. The primary concern of the leader is to maintain internal harmony within his lineage so that disruptions which would lead to segmentations are avoided. In this task he is aided by the strong patterns of deference to seniors which exist in the kinship system and by the patterns of inheritance which will make him trustee to his deceased brothers' property until such time as their sons are all adults. Shambalai may be seen as a congeries of such lineages of diverse origin which hold land, and possess a corporate system of responsibility, leadership, and ritual. These are weakly associated together by agnatic and cognatic ties, but authority does not extend beyond the limits of the localized minimum effective lineage.

Shambalai is far more than this, however, for the institution of sacred chiefship depends upon the recognition of authority relations which do not follow from lineage membership. By authority I mean the legitimate right to command others, a right which clearly resides in each royal chiefship. The extension of this authority through the continued segmentation of the royal lineage has led both to an ever-broadening territorial unity and to the development of a deep segmentary structure in the royal clan which provides the vehicle through which this unity is maintained.

Thus Shambala society is divided into two strata. Within each of these it is primarily kinship which provides the structure of authority, but between the two strata it is not. Here it is an explicit ideology of inborn fitness to rule with its assumption of inequality, of differential access to many prerogatives, and its claim to a monopoly on the exercise of legitimate force.

The authority of the chief is at once pervasive and limited. The chief may command that his fields be cleared, that his men go to war, or that some lineage must cease activities deemed offensive and pay fines for its behavior. Yet in all of these cases the chief must be sure of broad consent and agreement among his people as gauged by the assent and active cooperation of his councillors. Few chiefs have been in a position to ignore or override the views of their councils. Chiefs appear to be more concerned that they be consulted and asked to render decisions and most importantly that no other individual or group attempt to issue commands or coerce anyone than that the chief himself should issue commands for every joint activity, although no such activity should occur without chiefly assent.

The authority exercised by the chief seldom penetrates the corporate lineage, but in general treats lineages as units which may have relations with each other and with the chief. Thus the lineage retains a considerable measure of responsibility for the security and support of the individual. This quality of chiefly power may be discerned in all types of joint activity but it emerges with great clarity in the settlement of disputes. When disputes involve members of different lineages, the chief must act to settle the matter. But he does not take direct action against the individuals; rather, his power is brought to bear upon the lineages to which the individuals belong. Any fine exacted is levied against the whole of the lineage. It is left to the members of the lineage to concern themselves with the individual who has committed the offence and to bring sanctions to bear upon him, for this is a matter of the authority residing within the lineage. The chief deals primarily with the corporate entities; i.e. the lineages. Yet the chief claims a monopoly upon the use of force in all relations among separate lineages. They are not privileged to solve their own disputes: the chief exacts fines from both lineages involved in a dispute, should this dispute not be brought to his attention. That is to say, the royal lineage claims the right of jurisdiction. Furthermore, the major portion of the fines exacted is retained by the chief. The chief's relation to commoners may be direct but it is more often a relation of chiefly power to corporate lineage. Likewise the relations among chiefs are pre-eminently those of lineage segment to lineage segment. The power of chiefship stems from participation in the qualities of the founder of the royal clan which are received through inheritance.[1] Thus every chiefship which is the corporate right of some royal lineage must stem from a royal lineage of greater span and must be subordinate to that chiefship which is the right of the greater lineage. Lesser chiefships are merged into greater chiefships in a manner analogous to the merging of lesser lineage segments in a segment of greater ascent. The result is a structure of command in the state which is a reflection of the agnatic structure of the royal clan.

The traditional history of the formation of the state together with the genealogies which stem from it are here viewed as the charter which legitimizes these present circumstances. Within this body of history are the precedents for present action, the guidelines for the flow of authority and the explanation of current relations. The powers of the paramountcy may be explained in terms of the charismatic leadership of Mbega while the inheritance of this charisma by his sons accounts for their acceptance. At the same time, the dependence of Mbega on his companions and advisors for the wisdom of his rule and upon the invitation of the people for the recognition of his power is stressed. Thus not only is the leadership accounted for, but the directions it may take and the checks upon it are specified.

Attention is focused upon the chiefly hierarchy by the constant repetition of the Mbega tradition in its role as a statement of precedent in the conduct of daily affairs. This is further reinforced by the ritual acts attendant upon entrance to the *kitala* and to the *nyumba nkuu*. This aspect emerges most clearly in the celebration of royal ancestor rituals in which the genealogical

---

[1] Max Weber, *The Theory of Social and Economic Organization*, translated by A. M. Henderson and Talcott Parsons (Glencoe: The Free Press and the Falcon's Wing Press, 1947), pp. 363-7. Weber here notes that the 'routinization' of charisma may follow several routes one of which is 'traditionalization', that is, that resting upon an established belief in the sanctity of immemorial traditions and the legitimacy of the status of those exercising authority under them.

connections of royal lineages are reiterated and in which the participation of commoners in the whole structure is stressed by their official roles in the ceremony. Finally, the participation of commoners in the boys' and girls' initiation ceremonies of the royal clan appears to have at least three separable but closely connected aspects. It is first an emulation of the action of a high status group towards which others are oriented and to whose values they aspire. It is also an explicit acceptance of the legitimacy of the position which the royal clan enjoys and a kind of oath of allegiance to the royal chiefs. Beyond this, however, it mirrors the power of the commoners, for it is mostly commoner functionaries who conduct the ceremonies and who possess the special magic to protect the ritual from evil magicians. No one denies that it is a Kilindi ceremony and that it 'belongs' to the chief, but at the same time the dependence of the chief on the ritual specialists who know the secrets of the ceremony is always heavily stressed. Of this relationship the people say, 'We are like the house poles of the house, its warmth makes us warm.'

Although belief in the inheritance of charismatic qualities is an important sanction for chiefly position which is reiterated in ceremony and bolstered by elaborate genealogies, it is a potential weakness as well as a strength. The maintenance of authority depends heavily upon genealogical connection, but if the attributes of chiefship are inherited within the corporate descent group of the ruler, there will be in every generation as many potential successors as there are men in the royal clan. At every death, the uncertainty of succession invites destructive conflict and intermittent weakness in the state.

In the particular conditions under which the Shambala found themselves in the nineteenth century, the potential tension over succession had the consequence of expanding the state rather than disrupting it. The absence of highly centralized political systems in the vicinity of the Usambara Mountains allowed the established chiefs to send out their sons or brothers as chiefs over less organized peoples, thus broadening the extent of the state rather than involving it in disruptive internal disputes over succession. The Alur display an exactly parallel process.[1]

However, this sort of process does not produce a strongly

[1] Aidan Southall, *Alur Society* (Cambridge: W. Heffer and Sons, 1956), pp. 181–228.

Conclusions

centralized bureaucracy. There is a supreme head, but there are also many lesser heads whose authority is essentially like that of the ruler since it flows from the same sources and cannot be viewed as delegated. The power of any chief depends upon his participation in the hereditary charisma of the royal clan and not upon closely defined legal competence in an hierarchical administrative staff. Since chiefships are the vested rights of lineages, they can only be viewed as appointive in an extremely extended sense. That is, they had to be founded by consent from above and the superior chief retains the power of ratification with regard to the accession of a new chief. In this case, the head of the system does not enjoy a monopoly upon the exercise of legitimate force but must in part depend upon the self-interest of heads of lesser segments to balance each other, and in part on the influence of commoner councillors who cannot assume the chiefship and so profit from maintenance of the *status quo* and not from war.

The councillor system, the power of ratification over chiefly accession, and the opposition among coordinate segments of the royal clan all act to direct power upward through the chiefly hierarchy. Thus although the corporate royal lineage has rights in a chiefship and does not depend upon the ruler for its claims to authority, the chief himself is bound to his superior through the ritual recognition of his chieftaincy and to his councillors for their support against rival claims to the chiefship. The likelihood of any royal lineage breaking away to found its own independent control is not very great under these circumstances. Even though the center does not enjoy a monopoly upon the exercise of force, its position is relatively secure in relation to lesser foci of authority.

Shambalai as a Political System

Fortes and Evans-Pritchard, writing in 1940, suggested a classification of political systems to which Shambala data are directly relevant.[1] The tentative scheme which they offered at that time divided societies into two major groups called respectively Group A and Group B. Group A included all those

[1] Meyer Fortes and E. E. Evans-Pritchard, (eds.), *African Political Systems* (London: Oxford University Press, 1940), pp. 5–23.

154

societies referred to as primitive states which they characterized by the presence of a centralized authority, administrative machinery, and judicial machinery (what they summed up as government, a point to which we must return). Group B was composed of all those societies which might be termed stateless and in which political relations were primarily regulated by a segmentary system of permanent unilineal descent groups.

They recognized a third type of those small societies in which political relations were coterminous with kinship relations, but they did not discuss it since such societies are extremely rare in Africa. However, it is of some importance that they provided such a category since it follows from the distinction between kinship and lineage organization which they have made and is important theoretically.

This typology has been extremely useful because it has stimulated interest in political organization among anthropologists and has led to a number of important empirical and theoretical contributions. Paula Brown offered one of the first of these in her study of authority in West Africa.[1] Here she was able to show that there were many 'stateless' West African societies in which associations rather than segmentary lineage systems regulated political relations and there were, furthermore, systems in which lineages were combined with other types of social entities in the regulation of political relations. It was clear from her analysis that the classification proposed by Fortes and Evans-Pritchard was inadequate as a typology of political systems, for the residual category of systems which did not fit was of very large proportions.

J. A. Barnes approaches the problem from a different set of empirical data which lead him to consider the use of the term segmentary.[2] He points out that although Fortes and Evans-Pritchard use the term to refer exclusively to lineage segments, it may equally apply to Ngoni residential segments which are not solely composed of lineage mates although they have a unilineal core. Further, many other societies may be conceived in terms of segmentary units because they share the property of

[1] Paula Brown, 'Patterns of Authority in West Africa', *Africa*, Vol. 21, pp. 261–78.
[2] J. A. Barnes, *Politics in a Changing Society* (London: Oxford University Press, 1954), pp. 48–9.

continuous subdivision through time into politically opposed and discrete units subsumed within larger units of a similar character. Thus in Barnes' view the concept of segmentary organization must be broadened to include systems in which articulation is not only upon the basis of unilineal descent but also upon the basis of other structural principles. Empirically then, there are states such as the Ngoni in which the segmentary process occurs even though a hierarchy of administrative positions is also present. Fortes and Evans-Pritchard were certainly aware of this at the time they wrote, for Fortes has elsewhere said that 'it is quite possible for the sub-divisions of a centralized state to have a segmentary social organization'.[1] Indeed such a situation exists in the case of the Bemba considered in the body of the book to which Fortes and Evans-Pritchard were supplying a theoretical introduction.

In a later publication, Fortes went on to acknowledge that lineages might have important political functions in a centralized system, but he nevertheless viewed such systems as inherently unstable and did not consider such societies as segmentary.[2] It is precisely this point that Barnes' data on the Fort Jameson Ngoni brings into question, however, for the continuous process of segment fission within the Ngoni state is not only a segmentation of unilineal groups, but also a subdivision of administrative powers. Furthermore, the system continued to function, unchecked by internal inconsistencies of any sort and only began to alter internally in any important way after the intervention of the purely outside power of European and Arabic exploration and administrative intervention.

Aidan Southall, writing at almost the same time as Barnes, addressed himself to this problem in very similar terms and identifies the societies characterized by the co-existence of segmentary organization and specialized administrative institutions as a clear-cut type which he labels the 'segmentary state'.[3] This type he identifies not only upon the basis of the presence of a continuously segmenting system but also upon the identity of

[1] Meyer Fortes, *The Dynamics of Clanship among the Tallensi* (London: Oxford University Press, 1945), p. 234.

[2] Meyer Fortes, 'The Structure of Unilineal Descent Groups', *American Anthropologist*, Vol. 55, No. 1 (1953), p. 26.

[3] Aidan Southall, *Alur Society* (Cambridge: W. Heffer and Sons, 1956), pp. 246–9.

powers exercised at the various administrative levels. This is a distinction of considerable importance, for it is precisely this which differentiates the Shambala or Alur systems from that class of states in which administrative function is so specialized that certain areas of authority are reserved to the top of the administrative hierarchy and lesser powers are distributed in graduated form to the lower levels where they are regarded as delegated from the center.

Southall also regards the grading off of the power of the center as distance from the center increases as very important, but this does not seem crucial, for it must be true in any political system based upon a relatively simple technology and cannot be regarded as diagnostic of only the segmentary state. It is nevertheless important since it allows the peripheral foci of power to maintain themselves with more ease than would be the case under rapid communication. Paradoxically, the strength of a state like Shambalai resides in the identical derivation of the authority of every royal chief. The maintenance and validation of authority is here accomplished without rapid communication by a focus upon mythical and genealogical sanctions. The ultimate difference between this and other state systems is the essence of segmentary structure, the contraposition of structurally like elements which combine the administrative function of the exercise of authority with the political function of power competition. The pyramidal form that it assumes is based upon the oppositions between coordinate segments which in turn are merged by the oppositions of segments of higher ascent, and finally by their joint opposition to surrounding groups which are outside the system. As has been previously suggested, the center cannot and does not claim a monopoly upon the exercise of authority but must operate in a field in which it depends upon the oppositions among lesser foci to give it overwhelming force. Of this relationship the Shambala say, 'The brothers who beat each other, they are two. The one who stops it is the third.'

M. G. Smith has offered a very rewarding approach to the analysis of such systems in a long essay which examines the logical basis of segmentary theory.[1] Here he shows that within

---

[1] M. G. Smith, 'On Segmentary Lineage Systems', *Journal of the Royal Anthropological Institute of Great Britain and Ireland*, Vol. 86, No. 11 (1956), pp. 39–80.

segmentary lineage systems there is a coincidence of administrative and political action. As Smith puts it,

> ... this simply means that in a lineage system, relations between superordinate and subordinate lineages are normally administrative and based on authority, whereas relations between coordinate units are normally political and express relative power. Since the dimensions of lineage organization embrace superordination and co-ordination together, and since it is in these dual terms that the position of any segment of the structure is defined, this simply means that each segment is latently or actually involved in simultaneous contraposition and subordination with reference to at least two other segments.[1]

This coincidence of elements leads Fortes and Evans-Pritchard to view lineage relations as expressing political behavior which is indeed the case. But it also leads them to deny the existence of government in such societies since specialized offices vested with authority do not exist and thus to make a dichotomy between state-type centralized societies which exhibit an hierarchy of administrative offices (government in their terms) and acephalous segmentary societies which do not. In Smith's terms this is not a dichotomy but rather a continuum along the axes of administrative and political action.

There are cases in which there is a rather high degree of coincidence of administrative and political functions in the same concrete social entity as is true of the Tallensi, Bwamba, or Gusii. Yet even in these systems there is some differentiation of administrative office from segmentary unit as for example, the *na'am* chiefship of Tallensi which is importantly, but not completely, defined in terms of lineage structure.[2] Cases such as the Shambala seem of considerable importance in these terms for here there is somewhat more differentiation of specialized administrative office from the lineage structure in which it is nevertheless still embedded. As M. G. Smith makes clear, political and administrative behavior are analytically separable and it is the task of an empirical study to discover how they are combined or separated in some particular concrete social entity or series of such entities. The Shambala as a case in point

[1] Smith, *op. cit.*, p. 52.
[2] Meyer Fortes, *The Dynamics of Clanship Among the Tallensi* (London: Oxford University Press, 1945), p. 43.

display a structure in which the ideology of rank combined with that of unilineal descent is reflected in differentiation of governmental action of segments.

Societies possessing this combination of features are by no means rare in Africa as has been recognized by a number of writers. Both Gluckman and Southall have listed numbers of societies displaying such structure. Indeed segmentation and the definition of segments is an essential process of political action in all societies. In some cases, there also exists an ideology of unilineal descent such that lineages may form a basis of governmental organization either in combination with other administrative and political structures or without them. Lineage principles and structures are associated with rank and office in Shambalai in what was an expansive and successful state.

That such systems are unstable as Fortes has held may well be the case. As Smith observes, 'Under such circumstances, also, tendencies emerge favouring the specialization of units in political or administrative function.'[1] Southall expresses the same view in another way.[2]

> Segmentary states are, indeed, fragile structures of great flexibility . . . Transition . . . must be associated empirically with such factors as the decreasing efficacy of ritual powers, the abolition of the feud system, the definition of feudal obligations, fiscal development, royal landholding, and the general elaboration of the bureaucratic idea especially as concerns the passage from hereditary subordinate authorities with generalized political powers to transferable officials with restricted and closely defined powers.

They may persist, however, over long periods of time for the ideology which informs the structure is amenable to accretion, amalgamation, and adjustment and is not thus destroyed just as the ideology of kingship is not destroyed by usurpation or rebellion. As the Shambala put it, 'New arrows, make them like old ones from the *kitala*.'

[1] Smith, *op. cit.*, p. 53.   [2] Southall, *op. cit.*, pp. 260-1.

Appendix

HABARI ZA WAKILINDI[1]
(THE HISTORY OF THE KILINDI)

ONE of the aims of this study is to investigate the manner in which the image a people has of its culture is utilized to inform the behavior in which they engage. The Shambala possess an explicit and detailed image of their state which is rooted in traditional oral history and the mass of genealogies and legal cases which they fit into that traditional history. Malinowski argued many years ago that myth acted as a charter which expresses and codifies belief and I found great force in that view as I observed the lives of the Shambala whom I knew. The story which I have abridged here is an exciting account of a man's life told with pomp and splendor but it is also an explanation of the ties which hold the chiefdoms of Shambalai together, a justification for their fealty to the king, a vouching for the efficacy of the rituals they perform, and a tribute to the power and glory they have known.

I do not know how much of this history is based in fact, or indeed if any of it is. It is nonetheless real in that special sense of cultural reality, which makes what men believe the moving force of their actions and the reference for their lives and decisions.

Of old time there was in the country of Uzigua above Nguu a man named Mbega. This man was in strife with his kinsfolk. [They said of him, he is ill-omened and if he does not leave our country we are determined to kill him though we do not relish to shed a man's blood.] . . . Now Mbega had a craft; he hunted wild pigs with dogs in the forest; and by that craft he got food

---

[1] I am indebted to Mr. J. W. T. Allen for permission to make this abridgement of his and his father's translations of *Habari za Wakilindi* which first appeared in *Tanganyika Notes and Records* and is soon to appear in full for the first time in a new translation by Mr. Allen.

and clothing. And he had many companions who followed him; . . . All these companions loved Mbega, and others of the people, all except his brethren, loved him . . . Even the chief held him in great respect, and day and night he was busy with men's affairs. Now God had given him grace of person and of speech, and knowledge of healing charms; if any was sick he healed him; and charms for war he knew, and to protect the town he could use magic, and wild beasts did not catch either men or goats or fowls. So Mbega was indeed a very great man in the country. He dwelt among the people and if war arose he worked charms and the war was ended, and if a sudden attack was made on the town, he made magic and covered all the town with clouds like smoke, and their enemies sought for the town and could not find it, and they departed and went their way. So Mbega was a very great man.

[Once there was a hunt planned when few pigs were to be found near the town because of the hunting, and for two days they searched and] . . . In the morning [of the third day] they said to Mbega, Today let us go to that forest of which we spoke in the town, and if we do not find them, we had better go back. So they set out . . . and found pigs . . . The dogs rushed at them and scattered them . . . the noise made by the pigs was like the roaring of lions, and some of the men climbed up into trees and others fled at the sound of the pigs charging the savage dogs, for the turmoil was terrible. Five men were hurt and the Chief's son was killed . . . When the men came together again they found the Chief's son dead, and they said, What is to be done? This is the son of great people. Mbega said, I shall do what you think best. They said, There is nothing for us now, but to flee wherever we may . . . Mbega asked, Do you think that where we are going, the Chief cannot follow us and catch us? His companions answered, Do not let us think that; a fugitive does not heed darkness, sunlight is not for him; so we must not heed darkness or danger. Mbega said, That is true. They set off, fifteen men . . . They went along those hills [and] they built little huts and they lay down there. On the next day the men of Zirai saw smoke by day and fire by night, and they said, Perhaps that fire is men of Kombora looking for honey. The second day and the third they saw the same thing, and they said, Let us look into that fire in the bush. Eight men set out . . . and they

came and watched . . . [and] they asked, Strangers whence
came you? They said, We are hunters of wild pigs . . . [and
after much talk] Mbega went with one man to Zirai Pangai . . .
So Mbega dwelt in Zirai and every day he went hunting, and
wherever men heard of it, they came to buy flesh and to beg him
to go to their land to kill pigs; and he bought mortars and
pounding sticks and pots and all manner of household stuff, and
sent them to his companions there in the bush . . . And by his
grace, and justice, and magical powers gradually won the allegiance of the whole district of Bumburi. So the people loved him
and determined to give him a wife from one of their own villages . . . and all the people without dispute acknowledged him
as their chief.

Now when he was ruler of Bumburi tidings reached Vuga
and Turi its headman, that there was in Bumburi a great
magician, and that [he knew war charms, and that he could
bring clouds over the land, and that if any man was sick he
healed him. And Turi called all his people together and told
them all that he heard and that it was said that Mbega was] a
goodly person and compassionate; if a man is charged with
debt, and has not wherewith to pay, he takes of his own property
and pays, and now he has freed all the people of Bumburi. [The
people said,] Turi, if you wish to bring him here, send men to
spy out the truth about him. [These men went and they said to
men of Bumburi,] We want Mbega in Vuga . . . because we
have a great war with the people of Pare. Mbega said to the
elders, Tell them that if they want me, I would speak with their
headman . . .

Turi went out with the men of Vuga . . . and war horns and
flutes, and signal drums and five oxen as a present for Mbega
. . . They came to that place with . . . song and dance and
every man vaunted his prowess and glorified his country and
boasted of his pre-eminence and rank. [The men of Bumburi
went to Mbega and told him,] The headman whom you called
from Vuga is here . . . What shall we do? Mbega said, I have
heard his speech of triumph . . . I have heard all his words.
Are they true or false? They answered, What he said is true . . .
Whoever comes to this country of Usambara must admit that
he is Turi's man. That clan holds this country, because God
gave them the gift of working iron and skill in war . . .

. . . And Mbega met them but because the sun was exceeding hot he took his little gourd and made clouds rise from out of it and they covered the sky. . . . Even there where his guests were they felt the chill, and they thought, This man is too powerful for us . . . and they all greeted him courteously, and they bowed themselves before him with fear and kissed him . . . Turi said to him, Now I want you to agree to come to Vuga [and Mbega agreed after they accepted his conditions to build a house for his charms.] All was done as Mbega had ordered and the house was built . . . in a grove near Vuga where the headmen of Vuga were buried. Then at last Mbega went to Vuga taking with him his wife and one of her brothers. [On the way did Mbega kill a lion and they skinned it and he said, Take care, for I want to sleep upon it; I will not sleep on ox skins any more . . .]

In the morning they beat the war drum to call the people to greet Mbega, and when the people heard the sound of the drum they came in their multitudes, for the sound went throughout the land . . . Men came from all the towns and country round about, even from Bumburi and Zirai. An elder of Vuga stood forth and said, We saw a stranger come into our town last night . . . and we said, It will not do to discuss this matter without calling all the people. If we send messengers that will take many days, let us beat the war drum.

An elder of Bumburi stood up and proclaimed his name and title . . . and said, We entertained the stranger as a hero and wonder worker. When we received him we did not beat the war drum. You . . . coveted him and brought him here and we did not refuse.

Another man of Vuga spoke, saying, What have you said you man of Bumburi? You had good reason not to beat the drum. If you had, who would have attended? All men listen, all ears are towards Vuga; and this stranger now that he has alighted here has no other place to go. If any man wants the new story let him come to Vuga; if any is sick, let him come to Vuga; if any have law suits, let them come to Vuga. Every matter good and bad always comes to Vuga.

A man from Ubiri stood forth and said, Now cease this dispute and show us the stranger so that we may know him.

A man of Vuga led the way, and a man of Bumburi followed

him. After . . . came a man of Ubiri, and a man of Rungui, and after him a man of Mlalo and of Mlola, and after the man of Mlola, all the people of Usambara. They saw Mbega, his fine bearing, and the grace of his countenance, and his eyes, and his smile, and his stature; of all the men of Usambara there was not one who was up to him by half a head.

The men of Vuga said, He is our king without a doubt . . . The others said, We cannot help wanting him to be our king because of his craft and his beauty and his eloquence. A man of Vuga said, The matter is ended, he is our king . . . They brought him out in the courtyard to the multitude and took his hand to signify that he was indeed their lord, and they proclaimed, Every word that he says we accept, and if any man refuse, and he says, Let him die, we will kill him by universal consent. The whole assembly responded. Then two oxen were killed, and the people ate and took their leave and departed each man to his own place. So the men of Vuga dwelt with their king, and he governed and enforced the laws, and all the country brought their questions to him and he decided them.

[After Mbega had been in Vuga a short time he called Turi] and said, I want a large house, because [my wife is with child, and I see that her days are nearly fulfilled . . . Turi and the elders answered,] We have heard, we will set all the people of Vuga to work. [The people came and they did the work, and nothing was left undone.] And Mbega brought an ox and gave it to the doers of the work, and they killed it and divided the flesh and went home . . .

Now Mbega determined to move into the house . . . and he entered with his wife and when they went in the others departed. Then Mbega told one man to bring the skin of the lion, and he brought it; and Mbega said to his wife, Get up now upon the bed [where the lion skin is] and lie on it. Instantly his wife said to him, My pains are upon me, fetch a woman to come . . . Other women were called . . . and soon she brought forth a child safely . . . [and people came rejoicing with fine presents and sweet kernals and bananas.] . . . This child was called Simba son of Mwene [for reasons no man now knows].

The men of Bumburi say that after the birth of the child, the people sat down to discuss the matter, and they said, It will never do for the child to be brought up in the country of Vuga, for he will not get to know us his kinsfolk . . . [And very many of the elders of Bumburi went to Vuga to persuade Mbega to let his wife and son go home with them. After Mbega had spoken with his wife he said,] I like the plan, go to Bumburi and bring up the child there . . . And he prepared for them food for the journey and gave his son ten milch kine and very many goats, and he took leave of him in due form and gave him clothes, and he set out with guards and very many young warriors and much people, a great army without number . . . In the morning men went to Bumburi to report . . . and when the elders heard that they took counsel. They agreed, Let him go to Lukoka to the town of his grandfather.

Buge [the son's common name] came to Bumburi and was brought up there with all honour and was waited on, and had his field cultivated and his cattle pastured well, and whenever a case came before his uncles, if cattle were forfeited, he was given a beast. [And very many days passed and Mbega said, Now] I want to give you a man to watch over him and to live with him in the Great House in Bumburi till the boy is grown . . . Choose out a man of understanding and considerate character, not a covetous man, a good speaker and a man of courage, one who can walk from morning till night, not an overbearing man, not a man who can insult the child. [Then Mbega said to the men of Vuga,] I want to set up a man to be their leader and to govern them; so my son will have a judge among all the people . . . I sent men to search out the man, and they have found him, and now I want a man of Vuga to go to instal him in the Great House . . . [and he found a man and he went there and there came a great multitude of people.] Then Mbega's messenger held aloft a spear and gave instructions to the man, Dwell with the lad in all honour, do justice without respect for any man's person, even though it be your son or brother, judge according to the law.

At dawn that man brought an ox and they set the guard for him . . . and they went to show him the fields, and they killed a goat there, and they cooked bananas and they ate, and they instructed him . . . And the man of Vuga said, We will go our way; but if Mbega has any message for you he will send me, and if any other man comes . . . do not accept him, even if he bring the spear of Mbega.

After these things the men of Ubiri heard what had been done, and they gathered and took counsel together and they determined to take one of their children and send her to Mbega to be his wife, that they might gain the same benefits, for they said, If we send him our child, we shall get flesh every day, and honour; and if she gives birth, we will go and fetch our child and grandchild to bring him up here, and we shall get property and dignity. [And they made a plan and Mbega accepted their daughter and she went and dwelt there at Vuga.] And she conceived and bore a daughter, who died, and she conceived again and bore a son . . . The people of Ubiri came and took their grandchild to Ubiri [and he fell sick, and Mbega went out to Ubiri and took omens and saw that the child would not recover there and took him to Shashui and he recovered there.]

[When these boys were of the age proper to such things, Mbega ordered that they be circumcised and very many oxen were killed and there was much rejoicing and] the elders of Bumburi took counsel and [they determined to] ask the chief to let them instal the boy as chief there in Bumburi. [They met in Vuga] and they were asked their business. They said, We have come because we want to set up Buge as chief in Bumburi; he is grown up; the people have agreed to wait on him, they have agreed that he shall be their judge, they have agreed to till his fields and to plant them, and that men shall wait on him, each for two days. Mbega answered, If you are agreed on this, I too approve; but let me ask the elders of Vuga . . . The elders of Bumburi took leave of the chief and went home. [And the messenger of Mbega came to Bumburi and they beat the war drum and people came from afar and they assembled, a great host, and] the agent of Bumburi stood up and took the Sambara spear and the Sambara shield . . . and cried aloud, Hearken to me all you who are here present, our chief is Buge here, the son of Mbega . . . Then the man from Vuga took the spear and shield and going round the courtyard said, Hearken to me, your herald; if you see another man of Vuga coming and saying, I have been sent by Mbega with this or that message, if he does not have the spear which I now hold as his token, bind him; either [the] messenger must bring my token, or I must come myself. I have been sent by Mbega to come to give his son, lo! he is before you, hearken to him. If he does wrong, call me and tell me, and I will correct him; and if he does not listen, he shall be removed and his brother set in his place. Then they brought Buge into the courtyard and gave him the spear and the shield, and he held them aloft and [he was answered], *Muramba! Muramba!* [Then the herald departed and told the news to Mbega and Mbega sent word to Buge to come to Vuga].

They took three oxen and a hundred pots of cane beer and they took their spears and girt on their swords, and very many young warriors went with them, and they took horns and trumpets. A great host accompanied Buge to Vuga . . . and they entered the Great House which is called Burira. Buge and his father greeted one another, and the men of Bumburi cried, Simba Mwene! and Mbega answered them, Eeeee! The men of Bumburi cried again, Your son! and the herald said, Your son has brought three oxen as tribute. Mbega said, It is well, let them take them back to your house. Then he told his guards to take six oxen and give them to the elders of Bumburi. That night the Chamberlain of Vuga came and took the lad to the king's house and he took him into the house to show him the magic of the Sun, and very early in the morning he took him to the herald's house to rest. [And that afternoon the men of Bumburi departed from Vuga.]

So Buge ruled in Bumburi, and there was great peace between him and his brothers. One [brother] was Kimweri who was over Ubiri, one was chief of Mlalo, one was chief of Mlola, and one was chief of Mɪungui, and of all these Buge was the greatest.

The day of Mbega's death was known only to five elders . . . and his guards told any who came that the chief was detained by his magic . . . [and the herald went by night to inform Buge who came and stopped at the grove outside of Vuga where they buried Mbega according to their custom, wrapped in the hide of a black bull, and still the people in the town knew nothing. After that they took counsel and it was decided Buge should stay there in Vuga lest the news come to brothers and they seize Vuga.]

Whilst it was dawn yet orders were given that the great drum should be beaten . . . and the people took their weapons and came to Vuga. There they saw a great mourning . . . and wailing, now shouting, Buge is our chief. [The agent of Ubiri] held up his spear and . . . said, Officer of Vuga, we hear you proclaim Buge is Chief of Vuga. When did Mbega give the country to his son, and where has he gone? The officer took the spear and said, Our chief is dead; we buried him the day before yesterday; and he gave orders on his deathbed . . . to instal his son Buge as Chief in Vuga. [After this they all assented, they gave Buge his father's spear] and he raised it aloft and he was answered Mbogo! Mbogo! Then all the people went each to his own place, and Buge reigned in Vuga.

BIBLIOGRAPHY

ABDALLAH BIN HEMED BIN ALI LIAJJEMI, *Habari za Waklindi* (Sehemu ya kwanza, Sehemu ya pili, Sehemu ya tatu). Msalabani: U.M.C.A. Press (1901–5).

— 'Habari za Wakilindi' (Sehemu ya kwanza). *The Journal of the East African Swahili Committee*, No. 27 (1957).

ALLEN, ROLAND, 'The Story of Mbega', *Tanganyika Notes and Records*, Nos. 1, 2, 3 (1936).

BARNES, J. A., *Politics in a Changing Society*. London: Oxford University Press (1954).

BAUMANN, OSCAR, *Usambara und Seine Nachbargebiete*. Berlin: Dietrich Reimer (1891).

BROWN, PAULA, 'Patterns of Authority in West Africa', *Africa*, 21 (1951).

CAMERON, SIR DONALD, 'Native Administration in Nigeria and Tanganyika', *Journal of the Royal African Society*, Vol. 36 (1937).

COLONIAL OFFICE. *Native Administration in the British African Territories*. Part I. By Lord W. M. H. Hailey. London: H.M.S.O. (1950).

— *Report by His Majesty's Government . . . to the Council of the League of Nations on the Administration of Tanganyika Territory for 1927*. London: H.M.S.O. (1928).

COLSON, ELIZABETH and GLUCKMAN, MAX, eds., *Seven Tribes of British Central Africa*. London: Oxford University Press (1951).

CORY, HANS, *African Figurenes*. New York: Grove Press (1956).

— *Sambaa Law and Custom*. Revised and edited by E. B. Dobson. Unpublished manuscript on file at the District Office, Lushoto, Tanganyika (1946).

CORY, HANS and HARTNOLL, M. M., *Customary Law of the Haya Tribe of Tanganyika*. London: Oxford University Press (1945).

COUPLAND, REGINALD, *East Africa and Its Invaders*. London: Oxford University Press (1938).

CUNNISON, IAN, 'History and Genealogies in a Conquest State', *American Anthropologist*, Vol. 59, No. 1 (1957).

DANNHOLZ, J. J., *Im Banne des Geisterglaubens*. Leipzig: Evangelisch-Lutherishen Mission (1916).

DOBSON, E. B., 'Land Tenure of the Wasambaa', *Tanganyika Notes and Records*, No. 10 (1940).

EAST AFRICAN METEOROLOGICAL DEPARTMENT, *Summary of Rainfall for the Year 1955, Part II Tanganyika*. Nairobi: East African Meteorological Department (1955).

EAST AFRICAN STATISTICAL DEPARTMENT, *African Population of Tanganyika*

Bibliography

Territory. Nairobi: East African Statistical Department (December, 1950).

— *Quarterly Economic and Statistical Bulletin*. Nairobi: East African Statistical Department (June, 1952).

EICHORN, A., 'Beitrage zur Kenntnis der Waschambaa', *Baessler Archiv*, I (1911).

EVANS-PRITCHARD, E. E., *The Nuer*. London: Oxford University Press (1940).

FALLERS, L. A., *Bantu Bureaucracy*. Cambridge: W. Heffer and Sons (1956).

FITZGERALD, WALTER, *Africa*. 7th rev. edn. London: Methuen (1950).

FORDE, C. DARYLL, 'The Anthropological Approach to Social Science', *The Advancement of Science*, IV, No. 15 (1947).

FORTES, MEYER, *The Dynamics of Clanship among the Tallensi*. London: Oxford University Press (1945).

— 'The Structure of Unilineal Descent Groups', *American Anthropologist*, Vol. 55, No. 1 (1953).

— and EVANS-PRITCHARD, E. E., *African Political Systems*. London: Oxford University Press (1940).

GEARING, FRED, 'The Structural Poses of 18th Century Cherokee Villages', *American Anthropologist*, Vol. 60, No. 6, Part 1 (1958).

GOLDSCHMIDT, WALTER, 'Social Organization in Native California and the Origin of Clans', *American Anthropologist*, Vol. 50, No. 3 (1948).

GREY, SIR JOHN, 'Trading Expeditions from the Coast to Lakes Tanganyika and Victoria before 1857', *Tanganyika Notes and Records*, No. 49 (1957).

GULLIVER, P. H., *Alien Africans in the Tanga Region*. Unpublished manuscript in the Office of the Senior Government Sociologist, Arusha, Tanganyika (Sept. 1956).

HAMILTON, R. A., ed., *History and Archaeology in Africa*. London: School of Oriental and African Studies (1955).

JOHANSSEN, E., and DÖRING, P., 'Das Leben der Schambala', *Zeitschrift für Kolonialsprachen*, 7 (1915).

KRAPF, J. L., *Travels and Missionary Labours in East Africa*. London: Trubner and Co. (1860).

LANG-HEINRICH, F., 'Schambala-Worterbuch', *Abhandlunger des Hamburgischen Kolonialinstituts*, XXXXIII. Hamburg: L. Friederichsen (1921).

LASKI, HOWARD, *Grammar of Politics*. London: Allen and Unwin (1941).

LEVERETT, C. W., 'An Outline of the History of Railways in Tanganyika 1890–1956', *Tanganyika Notes and Records*, Nos. 47, 48 (1957).

LOWIE, R. H., *Primitive Society*. New York: Liveright Publishing Co. (1920).

MAC IVER, R. M., *The Modern State*. London: Oxford University Press (1926).

— *The Web of Government*. New York: Macmillan (1947).

MAINE, SIR HENRY, *Ancient Law*. 1st edn. The World's Classics. London: Oxford University Press (1931).

MALINOWSKI, BRONISLAW, 'Myth in Primitive Psychology', in *Magic Science and Religion and Other Essays*. Doubleday Anchor Book.

Bibliography

MOREAU, R. E., 'Suicide by Breaking the Cooking Pot', *Tanganyika Notes and Records*, No. 12 (1941).

MORGAN, LEWIS H., *Ancient Society*. New York: Holt (1877).

MURDOCK, G. P., *Social Structure*. New York: Macmillan (1949).

NADEL, S. F., *A Black Byzantium*. London: Oxford University Press (1942).

PAASCHE, H., *Deutsch-Ostafrika*. Berlin: No Publisher (1906).

POPPELWELL, G. D., 'Salt Production among the Wasambaa', *Tanganyika Notes and Records*, No. 8 (1939).

RADCLIFFE-BROWN, A. R. and FORDE DARYLL, eds., *African Systems of Kinship and Marriage*. London: Oxford University Press (1950).

REDFIELD, ROBERT, 'The Folk Society', *The American Journal of Sociology*, LII (January 1947).

ROEHL, K., 'Versuch einer systematischen Grammatik der Schambalasprache', *Abhandlungen des Hamburgischen Kolonialinstituts*. III. Hamburg: L. Friederichsen (1911).

ROSCOE, JOHN, *The Baganda*. London: Macmillan (1911).

ROYAL ANTHROPOLOGICAL INSTITUTE OF GREAT BRITAIN AND IRELAND, *Notes and Queries on Anthropology*, 6th rev. edn., London: Routledge and Kegan Paul (1951).

SMITH, M. G., 'On Segmentary Lineage Systems', *Journal of the Royal Anthropological Institute*, 86, II (1956).

SOUTHALL, A. W., *Alur Society*. Cambridge: W. Heffer and Sons (1956).

SPEKE, J. H., *What Led to the Discovery of the Source of the Nile*. London: William Blackwood (1864).

TANGANYIKA, *Annual Reports of the Provincial Commissioners on Native Administration for the year 1929*. Dar es Salaam: Government Printer (1930).

— *Report of the Mlalo Rehabilitation Scheme*. Unpublished manuscript on file at the District Office, Lushoto, Tanganyika. October (1949).

TAUTE, M., 'A German Account of the Medical Side of the War in East Africa, 1914-1918', *Tanganyika Notes and Records*, No. 8 (1939).

WEBER, MAX, *The Theory of Social and Economic Organization*. Translated by A. M. Henderson and Talcott Parsons. Glencoe: The Free Press and the Falcon's Wing Press (1947).

INDEX

Abdallah Bin Hemed Bin Ali Liajjemi, 79
administration, British, 14, 16, 22, 28, 29, 31, 62, 90, 91, 126; European, 15, 27, 91, 132; German, 12, 24, 25, 26, 27, 29, 31, 137
adultery, 108
agnatic relatedness, 2, 34, 35, 36, 152
agriculture mixed with herding, 11, 12–13, 14
Akida system, 26, 28
albinos, 102
Allington, 24
Almond, Gabriel, xiii–xiv
Alur, xiii, 153, 157
Amani Institute for tropical research, 27
amini (blood brotherhood), 74
ancestor worship, xviii, 21, 36, 42, 43–6, 59, 98; withholding of, 101; royal, 1, 46–9, 75, 86, 114–15, 152–3; royal, and political organization, 47
ancestral relics, 46, 58, 65, 110
Ankole, xxvi, xxvii
appeal, right of, xix, 115–16, 136
Arabs, xxx, 19, 20, 79, 133, 134, 137
articulation of state systems, xv, xvi–xviii, xxvii
Asantahene, xxviii
Ashanti, xi, xvii, xxviii
Asu, *see* Pare
authority, familial, 78, 100, 101–3, 104; parental, 54; political, 1, 2, 100; structure of, xv, xvii, xxviii, 1, 23–4, 78, 150, 152; *see also under* chiefs, lineages, Shambala society, villages
avoidances, 55–6
Aztecs, xxix–xxx

bachelor's house, 55, 61

Baganda, xi, xix, xxvi, xxviii, xxix
Ba-Ila, xxvi, xxvii, xxviii
bananas, 13–14, 86, 144, 145
Bantu-speaking peoples, 7, 10, 11
Barnes, J. A., xiii, 5, 155, 156
Baumann, Oscar, 24–5, 125, 134, 136, 137
bawa njama (court house), 124–6, 135
Beals, Professor Ralph, xxxvi
beans, 13
beating, physical, 101, 108
beer, 86, 119, 135
Bemba, 156
Berrange, Miss Beryl, xxxvii
Billa, son of Kimweri, 29, 30
Birdsell, Professor Joseph, xxxvi
birth, 102
blood brotherhood, 70, 74, 94, 123
blood feud, 110
Bondei, 7, 11, 17
Brainerd, George, xxxvi
breaches of the peace, 106
bride wealth, 13, 33, 53, 59, 93, 102, 107, 146–7
Brown, Paula, xiii, 155
Buganda, xxvii–xxviii
Buge, 81, 82, 164 ff.
Bumbuli (or Bumburi), 25, 80, 81, 82, 162 ff.
Burira (house for royal relics), 135, 167
Bushmen, xi

Cameron, Sir Donald, 28
caravan route, 20, 25; fees from, 136–7
cassava, 13, 14
cattle, *see* stock
census, East African, of 1948, 14–15, 16–17; of 1957, 15
Chagga, 25, 134
charisma, 2, 78, 103, 104, 152, 154

173

charter for authority, xv, xxxi, 1, 5, 22, 38, 39, 76 ff., 152
chengo (patrilineage), 43, 50, 105, 142
chief, the paramount, *see* paramount
chiefdoms, 22, 35; border, 120
chiefs, great, 2, 87–8; lesser, 2, 62, 88; relations between, 2, 3, 79, 104, 152; hierarchy of, xvii, 2–3, 5, 114–21, 152, 154; relation to commoners, xvii, 77, 86, 99, 119, 152; attributes of, 83–5; selection of, xx, 85, 90, 117 (*see also* succession); ratification of accession by higher chief, xx, 118, 154; installation of, 85, 118, 119; authority of, 3, 103, 151; powers, duties and prerogatives of, 104–12; power with respect to land, 112–13; checks on power, 77, 120, 121, 123, 138, 152; territorial control, 3, 113–14; degree of control, 119–21; decision making, 88, 121 (*see also* council); salaries, 25, 111, 132; wealth, 104, 112, 144–9; *see also* clients, fines, services, slaves, taxes, tribute, *zumbe*
chiefship, 77, 78, 101, 150, 152, 154; benefits of Shambala system of, 92–3
children, establishing legitimacy of, 33
cinchona, 27
circumcision, 94–5, 165; female, 95
'civitas', xii
clan, the royal: acceptance of hegemony of, 1–2, 76–7, 86, 97, 99, 103, 153; extension of rule of, 16, 22–3, 82–3, 91, 92; hereditary charisma of, 2, 5, 152, 154; segmentary nature of, 3, 40, 86–7, 150; separation of from commoners, xvii, 1, 121, 126–7; women of, 95, 96; and ancestor worship, 46, 47, 75; and present-day political opposition, 31; *see also* Kilindi clan
clans, commoner, 21–2, 35–6, 38, 42–3, 45, 86; generation depth of,

38; number of, 40; segmentation of, 38, 40
clients, clientship, xxvi, 13, 21, 123, 145–6
climate, 12
coercion, *see* force
coffee, 13, 27, 55, 144
collateral lines, merging of, 38, 65, 66
commoners, 1, 77, 86, 99, 117, 119, 121, 123, 147, 152, 153; *see also* council
communication, channels of, 1, 5
compensation, 104, 105, 110, 116, 141–2
Cook, Mr. John, xxxvii
corvée, *see* services
Cory, Hans, 96, 97, 115
council of commoners, xx, 81, 121–31; appointment to, 123, 129–30; role of in selection of heir to the paramountcy, 126; — and chief: theory of independence of, 123–4; harmony between, 131
councillors, 73, 117, 118, 119, 130, 142, 143, 151, 154; positions and duties of, 122, 124–5, 127, 128, 129; tenure of office, 126–7; dependence on chief for sources of income, 127; right to labour services, 123, 129, 135; — to the paramount: compulsory residence at the capital, 122; power and wealth of, 122–3, 127; drawn from powerful commoner lineages, 123. *See also* mdoe and mlughu
court cases, 49–51, 93, 101, 124, 160
courtiers, 122, 123, 135
courts, chiefs', 122, 123, 124–5, 128; legal, xix, xx, xxv, 124, 135–6; *see also* Native Courts
crops, 13; cash, 33, 54–5
cultural reality, 160
culture, limits of not coincident with social system, 17; *see also* Shambala culture
cursing, 54, 101–2